To Win 2

Frank Bangay
August 97

To Nicky I hope you
enjoy reading this book
Good luck with your own
poetry
          Best Wishes
              Frank

September 14th 1999.

Published in Great Britain, 1999
by **Frank Bangay**
Co-published by
Spare Change Books,
Box 26, 136-138 Kingsland High Street,
Hackney, London E8 2NS

* * * *

British Library Cataloguing-in-Publication Data
A catalogue record for this book is available
from the British Library

ISBN 0-9525744-6-2

Typeset by David Russell
at
Survivors Poetry, 34 Osnaburgh Street, London NW1 3ND

Distributed by Spare Change Books
AK: PO Box 12766, Edinburgh, EH8 9YE, Scotland
AK: PO Box 40682, San Francisco, CA 94149-0682, USA
Active: BM Active, London WC1N 3XX

All Illustrations are by the Author

Prayer

Winter utters a few murmurs
In the frosty afternoon air
As sun rays dance through the smoke
Evening comes
The sky lights up with an emotional red
The sun bleeds a little
For the passing day.
Dusk falls
Casting shadows
Casting shadows everywhere
We are weary from trying
But angry from the blows we took.
How can we articulate that anger
Into positive actions and words
To build a new world
Out of the ruins of this one.

Frank Bangay
Autumn 1985

Contents

OLD TIME FRIENDS

Old time friends
We meet again
In the park in the autumn twilight
Feet shuffling through brown leaves
Such a simple greeting.

Old friends
We sit on benches
With a loneliness
And a longing
Pulling our coats up against the cold
We think of the first warm breeze of springtime,
No our spirits aren't really lost
They just get buried beneath our despondency
Waiting for love to awaken them again.

And we think of the opening buds of springtime
And we dream of eternal summer evenings
And we sing to a rhythm of hope in our hearts
Keep on singing
Keep on singing.

Old time friends
Lost in sadness
We remember the friends who could not be with us
Though physically gone their spirits are strong
And we feel their love guiding us on,
So back to the world of the normal we went
And we tried to fit in once more.

Old friends
All of us
A little confused, a little weary
We return home from fighting in the war of the minds,
But we fought the best we could
We never really lost
We just learned about wisdom and experience,
Now we wait for peace to touch us with a gentle hand.

And through the darkened evenings
of our restlessness
We look to the waking colours of consciousness
And we sing to a rhythm of hope in our hearts
Keep on singing,
Keep on singing.

Old time friends
We keep looking back
Through the winter of our discontent
Old friends' sorrow fills us
As we hide ourselves and reflect.
Old time friends
Keep reaching out
Springtime is not so far away now
Old friends let us look forward now
To a youthful summer
Love will touch us somehow.

March 1990

Spring in the Park

3

Which Reality?

I

Sometimes truth appears like a dark shadow
Shrouding over all the hope we own
Muffled cries echo through the night
Perhaps they are trying to tell us something
That we don't want to know.

It frightens me how it is that Fascism
Can grow out of our frustrations
The little gangster man in the battered hat
Gets knocked down
And struggles to stand up again.

Scathed and abused
He learns how to live without compassion
He keeps fighting his way back up

Shouting "Enough, enough,
"ENOUGH"
"ENOUGH"
"ENOUGH'S
ENOUGH!"

And then he explodes with POWER.

And in the heat of the moment
The daily toil and trouble
Heartbeats drum up a rhythm of struggle
How can we turn that rhythm
Into a song of hope?

II

Trees stand naked and misshapen
Against a winter backdrop
Houses turn a frosty grey
Blending in with the sky.

A child waves to a snowman
Through a misty window
The snowman waves back
Tears falling from his eyes
As he begins to melt away.

Into springtime
The warm sun makes us feel a little calmer.
Through summer a scream of colour
Trees begin to take shape again.

Falling into autumn
We fight to stop our hopes from dying.
So as the spring skies start crying.
The child waits another year
For the snowman friend to reappear.

A thought
A spirit
A memory in the dark.
Words so precious they shatter so easily

We search.
We need.
A special friend
A guiding hand to ease the strain.

And in the heat of the moment
The daily toil and trouble
Heartbeats drum up a rhythm of struggle
How can we turn that rhythm
Into a song of hope?

March 1986

TONIGHT FAITH WON

When the sun sets over this grubby old town
And the rooftops seem to catch fire
And trees watch over us
Wise old spirits
Standing strong in an ever-darkening dusk time.
And over a jagged horizon
Of factory chimneys and gasometers,
Church steeples, houses, and high-rise blocks,
The sky burns red and gold,
Forcing its way through the smog.

And a golden ray of evening sunlight
Reflects on a grey brick wall
And everything seems beautiful
And everything is beautiful.

And grass and weeds grow through cracks
in the bricks
And on the pavement down below
The reflection of a face in a puddle
Tries to say a little about the future.
But when morning comes.

Try to fight against fading confidence
For a fighting mind will become strong
Do not fear for orders of preference
For orders are just there to protect a status quo
Where someone has to play a submissive role,
We will submit no more.

When the sun sets over this lonely old town
And birds commute home

Another day's work done
And traffic rumbles down the main road
A crawling convoy of tired bodies and emotions.

And we wonder
Will we be lonely tonight,
Alone with memories?

Sometimes happy
Sometimes sad
A song of hope is playing somewhere,
Listen, Listen,
Can you hear it?
The song of angels
Who have seen a little too much of the cruelty in this life.

Soft and naked is human warmth
So wild a proud heartbeat
Determined to survive
Weary arms reaching
Will there be a reward?
But when morning comes.

Do not fear threats and clouds of confusion
Something inside longs for a life that is happy and strong
So subtle a mind manipulation
Sometimes so subtle
That we can't work out
Just where it's coming from.
So you tell me I'm insane
Again and again
But I will keep rising up, you know.

When the sun sets over lonely rooms
Myth and reality fight each other for control.

Night passes,
Night passes,
But when morning comes,

When the sun sets over cornfields
Growing towards a harvest time
Chimneys of nuclear power in the distance
Threatening to stunt growth
But the harvest still comes.

Rise up, Rise Up,
The Wind keeps saying
Rise and believe in humankind,
Poppies growing along pathways
Corn and wheat flapping in the wind
Red the emotions of an evening sky.

But when the morning comes.
When the sun sets
Hear the calling of friends
As defeat and faith fight each other for control.

Tonight faith won.

September 1986

The above poem about faith and surviving was written in the autumn of 1986 following the Chernobyl disaster in Russia, when a nuclear power station there leaked. The authorities were saying how Britain's nuclear power stations were totally safe. But while one hopes for the best I wasn't so sure. At the same time the daily newspapers were full of non-factual reports and scaremongery. I know the daily papers like to sensationalise things. But I couldn't help feeling a bit freaked out by events. I wrote this poem as a way to find strength and fight back against the mind manipulation we are fed by those in power, and to celebrate surviving. Hence the last verse. This poem is also about surviving other life struggles. **July 1997**

In Prayer

Early Spring
A waking sun
Reflecting around a room
Dancing over plants
Different shades of green and blue,
Soothing another hangover
Softening the sharper edges of the day
And I wonder why I punish myself.

Another dawn
Buds and blossom
Cover windswept trees
Bent and shapen by the winter
Now in the approaching warmth
They find a little peace.

A moan and a grumble
A moan and a grumble
Helps to pass the time away
Morning comes with feelings of regret and sadness.

Can we believe in goodness
The spiritual side to our lives?
Or are there too many barriers
Between us and our hearts?

The false bravado of alcohol
I look for answers in a beer glass
Now as I wake up
Problems worry away in my mind.

Early morning
The sun reflecting
Butterflies dancing
Birds singing
Softening the sharper edges
But it's hard facing the sharper edges
It seems better feeling a little numb.

The psychiatric institution hangs over us
As we walk a little further on
We walk with uncertainty
Fearing that we might accidentally take a step back.

Who will be there to listen?
Who will help us should we stumble?
Can we turn good feeling into goodness?
Can we hear the music of our heartbeats?
Are you a soulful friend?
Will you try to understand?

Please tell me that I'm not alone in my prayers.

May 1993

Landscape with Someone Trying to Grow

A Landscape With Someone Trying To Grow

Spring is Rising

There will be peace in our hearts someday
Now that spring is rising
So sing it out loud
Because it's more than a dream.

There will be faith in our hearts someday
Now that the buds are opening
So sing it out loud
Because it's more than a fantasy.

Meanwhile
We travel a weary road
Over miles of moorland bleakness
And the spirit of the music
Gives us strength at times of weakness.

We cross many rivers
Building bridges out of optimism,
Cherry Blossom and Hawthorn Flowers
Help to soothe away the dark clouds.

All the time
There's a bomb inside our heads
Ticking,
Ticking,
Ticking,
Ticking,

On
Off
On
Off
On
Off
ON.

We try to stay cool
In case the explosion comes.

There will be peace in our hearts someday
Now that spring is rising

SO SING IT OUT LOUD

Make it real.

Spring 1976 *(adapted Spring 1994)*

Park Song

I saw you smiling in the park today
I nearly felt strong enough
To smile at you.
I saw you talking to yourself
In the park today
I nearly felt strong enough
To talk to you.

You were sitting on a bench
With your headscarf on
Your winter coat
And your woolly gloves.
You had that distant look in your eyes
I knew no pain could harm you.

I saw you crying
In the park today
I nearly felt strong enough
To cry with you.

You look at yourself
They say you're going mad
I look at myself
They say I'm going mad.

See all the sad men
All the bad men
As they search this world
For a future
They compete and hate each other

They are very confused.
I saw pigeons in the park today
They were taking a stroll
Through the afternoon

Little children were feeding them breadcrumbs
And they were grateful
For a little food.

I found my spirit
In the park today
I found a little hope this afternoon.

You look at yourself
They say you're going mad
I look at myself
They say I'm going mad
We look at ourselves
They say we're going mad.

We try to love each other
But instead we fight
We try to love each other
But instead we argue
We try so hard to prove ourselves
But so many times we lose.
Show me one of your sensitive smiles.
It's so reassuring to watch you
I saw you at peace
In the park today
And I felt at peace being with you.

1979 *(Lyrics to **Song by Fighting Pigeons**)*

15

Woman on a Park Bench with Birds

Fragments Part (2) Friendship.

A spirit sparks,
a spirit catches fire;
Yes we can truly fly,
we are superhuman?
take care of your wings.

Picking up the pieces
of a shattered mind,
im trying to fit this jigsaw
into a clear picture;
some pieces we can fit alone
some pieces will only fit
if we work together,
and help eachother,
and learn about
the high
of friendship.

Frances
Banaghan

THE LAUGHING FLOWERS

Never really felt so sad before
I try to reach myself through my craziness,
Never really felt so detached before
In precious moments of peace
I try to reach my feelings.

To see the laughing flowers
As they bend and sway in the wind
To see the uncertain sky as it constantly changes direction,
The grey and sombre colours that hang overhead
The hopeful patches of blue that come and then fade.

She comes and goes into the mist
And through the confusion she gently smiles
The sunrays of hope that shine through the clouds
Struggling to reach on down to a lonely heart,
To set a spirit free,
But you can reach me.

Never really felt this sad before
Something seems to brood
But something struggles to be born,
Never really felt so fearful before
I am shrouded
But a little daylight still enters in.

I walk through the park in a forlorn breeze
I hear the birdsong and the whispering of the trees
I talk to myself.

A manic season of rainshowers and harsh wind
And warm moments of sunlight
That give calm to a troubled spirit,
The sadness and turmoil
That constantly worries away inside
Perhaps it is the uncertain end of changing,
Something getting so distant,
Something else creating,
Something wild,
Something crazy.

And the bright patterns of the laughing flowers
Constantly shift in the wind
An unstable balance of happiness and sadness.

But will you try to reach me?

Spring 1988

I'm Dancing With Damaged Wings

When a wind of chaos blows through our lives
It pulls meaning apart
And in the aftermath we sit and wonder
How do you mend a broken heart?

A saddened chuckle echoes through the darkness
It's a survival instinct that we know
And we wonder
How did we lose sight of our world view?
The ideology we held so close?

Somehow our dreams slipped through shaking hands
How can we fit all the pieces together again?
Reaching out for someone,
Someone special to hold on to.

But how do we trust
When experience has taught us so much about suspicion?
How do we love
When we have been hurt so badly?
Which turning do we take on the road
forward from here?

A "madman" tries to compose himself
So that he can fit in once more with the crowd
He tries hard to make the mask fit
But it's not easy keeping a stiff upper lip

When there's so much to express
So much confusion and bewilderment
At being alone in this hostile world.
When a storm of people blow through our lives
They take, dictate, and leave us drained,
And in the aftermath we sit and wonder
How do we fill this emptiness again?

We tried to trust
Afraid of being alone on an island
We tried to love
Afraid that the wound would hurt so deeply
And sometimes we would wish
That we were brave enough to try again.

A "madperson" tries to be at one with the crowd
But you can't hide fearful eyes
The years of being singled out,
And you can't hide the worry lines
That run across your face
As you take your place in the competitive day.

But memories haunt in the deep of the night
Leaving the longing to open up and cry
And to understand the experiences
That changed the meaning of our lives,
We are damaged
But those experiences have made us wise,
Yes, we can be strong this time.

March 1992

The Sun was Shining
When We went Out

The Sun Was Smiling
When We Set Out
We Didn't Want to see
Dark Clouds In The Sky

A DIFFERENT RHYTHM

I know
I need
I feel
I care
For you
And I would like to share
But barriers get in the way.

I look
I see
So dear
An image of hope on the horizon
As I look out on to another stormy day.

Warm loving arms reaching out
But in our corners shadows shroud us
Dark thoughts filled with pain.

A sunbeam comes dancing
A spirit of hope
Giving light, trying to tell us
"It's alright; come out and face the day."

I know
We feel
So hurt inside
A battered ego tries to keep the spirit alive,
Needing someone to share with
The need grows stronger every day

You look into my eyes
But something makes you look away
A little sadness, something a little crazy
Who would love a madman anyway?

The water is rough how can we cross
To the other side where our logics can meet
I'm going to grow some wings and learn to fly
A wonderful feeling of letting go
and being free again.

A winter sun fools us so deceptively
In this lonely place
Summer can seem so far away
To be surrounded by the softness of leaves
And the feeling of peace.

We know
We need
We feel
We care
But how do we overcome these barriers
that get in the way?

We hurt
Ourselves
and
Each other
Once again,

To relate
And face
A little danger,
We try to be heroes
But fear gets in the way.

I'm chasing sunbeams, looking for a
brighter day.

October 1992

Mad?

Mad?
> Or just trying to express
> So many things
> Flying through the world
> On a pair of battered wings.

We talk in patois
We struggle to understand each other
Our struggles cause communication
problems
But it's our personalities that matter.
Please try to listen.

When I was at school
You got a clout round the ear
If you couldn't speak proper.

The teachers had their own hang-ups
But the smacks made it harder to learn
Many smacks later
And I still can't spell or speak proper Queen's
English.

But I don't care
I don't care
No I don't care
I don't fucking care.

Sometimes we're stressed out
Or lost in ourselves,
Sometimes we're drunk
And staggering about,
Sometimes we're tanked up on psychiatric drugs.

24

We mumble
We slur
We stutter
Thoughts get fragmented and scattered.

But things could still make sense
If only the human race had a little patience.

I look out
Through a smokescreen of deceit and lies.
I see an angry figure
Asking
Why do you try and protect me from the truth?
Why do you pass me by?

Mad?
          Or just trying to express
          So many things,
          My wings may be battered
          But I will keep flying
          I won't give in.

Many tongues chatter in conflict
Sometimes we dismiss each other
Because we see too many differences.

But I have pride
I will fly
I refuse to be pitied.

So tell me
Can we ever find the space to listen?

May 1994

THAT PLACE ON THE HILL

When I was young
We would often ride on a bus
Past that place on the hill;
There were pigs and horses
On the side visible to the public
The funny farm they called it.

We would make jokes about the place
And stare at the people
When they ventured out into the street
But fear made us keep our distance.

I would join in the jokes
Even though
I was a fucked-up schoolboy
Who was sometimes considered backward
Other times told to pull his socks up,
Like everyone else
I needed my scapegoats.

Unaware
I didn't realise
Who had heard of E.C.T. and Major Tranquillisers?
It's the way they are
I thought
So different from us
The crazy ones.

Some years later
In my mid-twenties
I got free board and lodging
In that place on the hill,
The world outside became a frightening place

Many hostile voices
Many impossible situations.

The animals had gone
But the buses still went past
The funny farm
Became a Mental Hospital
Became a Psychiatric Hospital
Became a Psychiatric Institution.

I found out about Major Tranquillisers and E.C.T.,
Scheming psychiatrists
The authority figures
We are taught to look up to
Now they become symbols of fear.

The Psychiatric Institution became a prison
When there seemed no way out
No hopeful tomorrow
The world outside mocked and discriminated.

Praying for strength,
Someone to trust,
A helping hand,
A friendly face,
It becomes easy for any of us
To want to seek refuge
In that place on the hill.

I struggled on
A little damaged
I found wisdom
A sense of awareness
That I can sometimes communicate,
I value what I have learnt from surviving.

February 1995

FRAGMENTS: PART I

Childhood
So often a struggle
Daily fears
A fight for survival.

Pick of the Pops on the radio
On a Sunday afternoon
Shone a little light through the gloom
A hopeful rhythm,
As you worried about school on Monday.

Pudding basin haircuts got you
scapegoated
Wiping your nose on the sleeve of your blazer,
A school cap
That gets thrown over the railway bridge
And you got told off the next day.

It sometimes seemed safer
To be a bully
Than the frightened schoolboy
Who gets bullied,
There was a macho bravado
In being sent to the headmaster for the cane.

Grey shirt
Grey trousers
Grey just like the stiff upper lip
Grey just like the English weather so often is.

There were many walls
Many warning signs,
Keep out
Do not trespass,
But school became an institution
That you often felt trapped inside.

There are fragments
Fading photographs
Putting on slideshows inside the mind
A jolt from the past brings out detail,
A little colour creeps in.

Like a day on a summer holiday
When it didn't rain
And everybody enjoyed themselves.

May/June 1995

PART II

Once upon a time Tesco's sold clothes
It was the most unhip place to go
Outside school
When wearing Tesco's Bombers
You could feel a bit of a misfit.

Cool kids wearing Levis
'John Lee Hooker' written on the back of their Parkas
Rhythm and Blues records and cigarettes
You wanted to be like that.

Surviving
Seeking wisdom
The rebel struggled for self-expression,
Sometimes you learnt to accept **loneliness**
Can we value what we learn?

When you were lucky
And got a pair of Tesco's Jeans
Perhaps a jean jacket,
Not wanting to feel an outcast
You pretended they were Levis
And hoped that you never got **caught**
Being taken into Tesco's.

September/October 1995

Part III

It's Friday evening
Rushing home from school
Hoping that you hadn't got into **trouble**
Ready, Steady, Go on the television,
The revolution started here for **a struggling**
schoolboy.

John Lee Hooker,
Muddy Waters,
Howling Wolf,
A little liberation for a repressed **generation**
Struggling for release.

Then your superiors came into the room
"What are you listening to that for?"
"You need your brains tested."
"We fought in the war"
"So that people like that"
"Could come over here and take everything."

The Prefabs,
The Bomb Sites,
Echoed what your superiors were saying
Many were the grim reminders,
They knew best,
Did they know best?

The thud crash jangle of Rock and Roll
Against the noise and shouting
A gulf so wide
And full of fear.
But it's Friday evening,
Ready, Steady, Go on the television
A struggling schoolboy finds a little liberation
And hopes his superiors don't come into the room.

September/October 1995

Growing Up

Growing Up

Pornography

Your betters say wanking will drive you mad
That masturbation is evil
And unclean,
You get confused
Something starts rebelling.

Scruffy schoolkids feeling big
We looked at dirty magazines
Risking a caning
And many threats
From bitter teachers,
What were their perversions?

A mixed-up boy
Trying to understand
The meaning of approaching Adulthood
I would go to the second-hand magazine shop
And look through the *Penthouses* and the *Parades*.
Buying some with my pocket money
I smuggled them home
Hoping they were never discovered.

"Stay away from dirty women"
Was a much-heard warning back then.
During teenage years I worked in a warehouse,
A lorry driver sometimes brought in hard-core stuff

That we looked at during our tea break.
Older men turning the pages
With nicotine-stained fingers
Fags hanging from their lips,
Senior Service, Capstan Full Strength,
Coughing and spluttering
Ash falls on their clothes
Grubby laughter between puffs.

Wide boys boasting
About the birds they pulled last night:
Twenty pints and they can still get it up
And you're so young
You wouldn't know where to put it.
Misguided I wanted to be like them -
Drunk and foolish.

April 1996

HE SEES, HE FEELS,
IT'S JUST ONE OF THOSE THINGS

It was just one of those things
He was filled with remorse
when things didn't work out
and filled with guilt
when they did.

He sees her
he tries to make contact,
but the voices of others
argue inside his head;
then she laughs
and goes away -
not the kind of man
to fulfil her conditioned needs.

He sees her
in a pornographic magazine
Penthouse, *Mayfair*, or somewhere,
Cast in a dream setting
that seems so inviting
but a little unreal.
Looking for her hero
to be her lover
(or so the caption read)
but he knows that could never be him,
For heroes are macho
and a little bit dumb.

He sees her,
dressed in culture
at some cultured event,
Looking for a man
of good intellect
to have the right answers
to the holiest of questions -
someone to impress.
But he knows that could never be him,
for they say
genius is pain,
and he has enough damn problems
as it is.

And he is an angry man
but he tries not to be bitter
though sometimes he thinks
he is a failure,
saying it's just one of those,
just one of those things.

For he sees her in glossy colour
and in negative white and black,
just a projected image
on a darkened night-time street,
he feels, he needs.

He sees her there
in the day
on a crowded street,

her clothes, her hair,
and he sees her face;
she always seems to smile at him
but his conscience tries to tell him
that it is only make-believe.
Can he understand it?

He sees her,
in the pub,
at the striptease show,
up on the stage
taking off her clothes,
acting out his fantasies;
but she has her defences,
so he just peeps.
For she is an actress
acting for the macho beerguts
and frustrated men;
you can look
but you cannot touch . . .
and there is so little feeling.

He sees her -
alone in his bedroom
while he stares at the wallpaper
she arrives from his imagination -
then he hears the voices
of rebellion, morality, authority,
and taboo,

all arguing away
in a state of confusion.

He sees her,
He sees her,
he tries to keep control -
not knowing that one day
he might let go.
He hears the liberators
arguing about sexism,
but from where he is at
it's very difficult to understand these things.
And the situation he is in
could have happened to anybody -
he tries to care, he tries to feel . . .

He is sometimes a bitter man,
a little confused and frustrated
and sometimes a little too sensitive.

October 1985

TOUGH GUY GETS SENSITIVE

Sitting in a pub listening to aggressive men
As they shout after too much beer
"Who's got the biggest
  Most powerful dick
  Around here?"
"Which one of us is the biggest
  bullshitter?"

He pretends not to be afraid,
Has another drink
"Yes, I'm brave;
  A few more pints and I can join in."

Watching a woman on the other side of the room,
Such a shapely figure;
He eyes her up.
Feeling a tingle in his smelly socks,
He says he loves her
And that she fancies him,
But really he's pissed.

Jilted on too many occasions
Alone with his fantasies,
Deep inside
He needs,
He feels,
He tries to grieve.

"Can I banish misguided thoughts
  From my troubled mind?

But no:
I let my fantasies run wild,
I can't seem to stop."

Tough
Bottling it up
Hurt
But afraid to show it
He suppresses a tear
As it struggles to be free
And run down his cheek,
There's too much to lose by admitting to fears.

Deep inside, sighing
Outside lying
Night after night staggering home from
the pub
Through hostile streets
How much longer can he carry on like this?

A tough guy
Afraid to be sensitive
A feeling guy
Trying to be sensitive
He struggles with himself
Which side will win?
Will he ever learn the true meaning of courage?

September 1997
(A love poem for the macho man who is trying hard to change)

Tough Guy
Gets Sensitive

WHEN A MAN CRIES

Slowly

Breaking down the barriers
That seemed like impenetrable walls
The pain is starting to fade
It's getting a little easier now.

He feels tears start to water in his eyes
Then
One
Falls
Down
His
Cheek,

Then another,
And he starts to feel more understanding towards
others
Who are vulnerable
Like he is beginning to become.

When a man cries
He tries not to feel ashamed
Though the stigmas are hard to fight,
He just needs a friendly voice
To tell him that it's alright.

Pent up

He screams out that macho role
Conditioned by so many years,
In pain he tries to confront all those inbuilt
fears.

He tries
First
In
Anger
Then in frustration
Until the violence is gone,
Though others may laugh
He feels more sensitive now,
and his conscience feels strong.

When a man cries
He frees his heartache
Though the laughter of others never
seems to stop
Deep inside he knows he is right
And that his persecutors are wrong.
A little hazy now
He recalls a lonely room
That he returned to at the end of
troubled days
Where he fought depression
And depression always tried to win
And all around the world went wild with rage.

Where people twisted each other's arms
Oblivious to the pain
Until it became impossible to understand
Just what the hurting was,
He remembers the smell of stale beer,
Those lonely fantasies
That he could never communicate or
share.

Then he begins to recall
The words of compassion that came,
How he started to walk down a different road
Never wanting to return to the scene again.
When a man cries
He feels a little uneasy
Though his faith is becoming strong
He needs a friendly voice
To tell him that there is nothing to be ashamed of.

Gently

We learn how to comfort each other
We reach for tender moments that we can share,

Friend

Can we seek freedom and acceptance
In this stigmatised land?

Try to ignore those laughing faces
Soon their taunts will fade,
Let our confidence win over those accusing fingers
Soon their accusations will mean nothing

When a man cries
He feels so much stronger in his spirit
And sensitive in his soul,
Crying is hard to do
It takes a lot of courage
Can we try?

September 1984

Figure by a River

We Got To The River,
The Great Big River
It Was A Long Way
To The Other Side
Time To Reflect.

EB
April '96

In Loneliness

So those unpleasant memories come back to haunt us
Time and time again
Always a burden on my back
A demon always grinning,
You say it's impossible to live like this
Yes friend I can understand what you say
I too have had my share of impossible situations.

A lonely man spends his days
Staring at the walls of his room
Wishing he had someone to cuddle
And to tell his troubles to.

But as days go on
He gives up hoping
And spends his time staring at the wall
Wishing that the wall would open
And let in a little love.

Liberated people laugh
And say he doesn't try
But it's not his fault that his face and personality
Doesn't fit in
So he is always left struggling.

But this struggle
Is a struggle to believe in ourselves
And have faith in the positive things we try to do
Living is all about finding confidence
Come on, let us try to believe.

So it seems it will be another clear blue day today
Not a cloud to bother us in the sky
But we say we never see it like that
We say we always wake up feeling depressed.

We try so hard to see things a little clearer
We try so hard but that dark cloud gets more real
We try so hard to make believe that our spirits can fly.

How we cling to each other in loneliness
Or we search for a substitute for love.

We find a little warmth
We try to share it,
We find the flame inviting
We try to rekindle it.
We find a little empathy
We try to share that too,
Others would want to take that empathy away
But they don't understand
They haven't been hurt in the same way as us.

A lonely man gets up from his bed
There is a lonely woman somewhere
In his imagination she holds out her hand to him
And he holds out his hand to her
Hoping that one day they will hold each other.

August 1994

I'm Dreaming of You

48

WHEN WORDS OF
FRIENDSHIP ARE SPOKEN

A deserted beach
A figure walks
Lost and alone
Miles of sea and mystery
A future so unknown.

Is it a crime
To want those things in life
That make it all worthwhile
A reason to have faith
A reason to smile?

I stand in fear
Facing the day
So many impossible situations
So much I'm unable to say.

It's hard to show your feelings
It's hard to embrace
The one you feel so close to
How can we be that brave?

A deserted beach
Another sunset
Reflecting on the sea
Twinkling stars
A moon that watches
Cold and serious.

The macho man looms over us
A dark shadow in our lives,
He brings pain and bitterness
He hurts us all the time.

If I could shut off for just a while
From the ugliness in the mind
And reawaken beauty
I know she's sleeping deep inside.

A deserted beach
A figure walks
Lost and alone,
Looking out into the sea
A future so unknown.

Why is it so difficult to reach
The things that make life worthwhile?
To have faith
And embrace those possibilities
Friend, can we try?

February 1994

Figure on Beach

Fear

You tell me I frighten you
Well I never intended to
It's just my emotions trying to run free.

I'm not a tough man
I don't bully to impress
And there are many times when I'm afraid
There are many things that I am frightened of.

I'm afraid of strangers on night-time streets
I'm afraid of isolation,
I'm afraid of my superiors,
I'm afraid of love,
Afraid of death,
Sometimes I'm frightened of starting a new day,
And sometimes I'm frightened of you my friend.

But I know this is hard to understand
Because you are just human like me
Just a victim of inhibited society.

1974

THEY SAY, THEY SAY

They say beauty comes in glossy packages
But all I see is a frighted girl in warpaint
They say that monsters have no feelings
But I saw a monster crying the other day
And I saw a man hit somebody
While smiling all over his face.

They say that some have
And some have not
But who has the right to judge
And who really deserves to take the blame
And you tell me this land of ours is free.
Why then do you look at me in that way?

SEPTEMBER 1981

IN THIS STRANGE LAND

What good would it be
If I felt ashamed to show you my face
Living as a 'mental patient'
Always seen as a disgrace,
At the bottom of society
Always being denied,
Always being denied.

Us odd people
You see us everywhere
Out on the fringes
Learning how to survive in despair
Are we so unusual?
There's a communication problem in the way
Perhaps if you listened
We would make a lot of sense.

How much do you value me?
If I'm unable to communicate
Always referred to as a label
Never as a human being,
Talked about and patronised
How much do you care?
Portrayed as a problem
Never as a person,
We are not monsters
But individuals with feelings.

Us strange people
We hide in our ghettos

Given drugs that shape us to fit the stereotypes
In exchange for our thoughts and emotions,
Inside we suppress
So much
So much,
We long to express
So much
So much,
What is normal?
Just a word
Just a word.

What good are we
If we struggle for acceptance
When we are painted as evil or dangerous
In many a film or television programme,
But we
are scapegoats for 'sane' fears
Things that are shut away
So many suppressed tears

Just people making money
Out of vulnerability and troubled minds
Distorted media images
Newspaper diatribes.

Drugs that make our mouths taste of chemicals
We become impotent inside
Drugs that distance us
Into a disorientated world,
How can we relate to each other
In such a strange land.
But force and brutality
Abuse and chemical research
Do not solve our problems
They just make the pain worse.
What do they care

The MAD
The MAD
They say,
We go through life in masks
In time those masks start to crack.

Why don't you listen to our wisdom
The hope we find in survival
Listen, Listen,
So many expressive voices.

Us saddened people
Our spirits get so bruised
As we fight to believe in ourselves
Against condemning professional views.

Farewell scorn and mockery
The rebel stirs inside
The need for a warm human being to relate to
Someone who will listen
And try to understand
Sometimes an angel comes with a healing hand.

March 1993

This Poem was written after watching a television programme
and reading some newspaper articles by Marjorie Wallace from
SANE (*Schizophrenia: A National Emergency.*) They approach
things from a very negative viewpoint, and in so doing create a
lot of negative stereotypes. In this we are often judged as
people who will be a danger to ourselves and others who will
need to be continuously watched, controlled and denied their
freedom. This in turn causes people who have been labelled as
Schizophrenic to receive a lot of hostility from society. Also,
very little is ever said about the abuse we receive from
psychiatry and from society. I wrote this poem in the first
person because I felt personally threatened by the television
programme and the newspaper articles.

August 1997

Face Surrounded
by Staring Eyes

A FAIRY TALE

It was approaching Christmas in Nutwood. There was snow on the ground. It was cold but with a sort of warm glow all around. There was a buzz in the air. Rupert the Bear and his mates were standing round a bonfire singing Christmas Carols All of a sudden a UFO landed and some friendly Martians got out. They came up to Rupert and his mates and shook hands. Then they joined them round the bonfire singing Christmas Carols and traditional Martian songs.

Nutwood really exists. It is a village in a secret valley hidden in the Welsh Mountains. It is a magical place with many Ley Lines running through it, and many Crop Circles all around in the fields.

Wood Imps dance about in the woods eating little mushrooms that grow on the ground. Seeing such wonderful things, Goblins hang out in the wood leaning against trees drinking cans of Tennants Super. Goblins aren't really bad people. They are just misunderstood, the Punk Rockers of Fairyland. Nutwood has been totally unspoilt. Up until now that is. But recently the Tories have found out about Nutwood. Soon they are planning to spoil it all by building a motorway right through the town. It will tunnel through the mountains and come out in Cardiff or somewhere like that. And the property developers are moving in and are planning to build a shopping centre, complete with a McDonalds in it. But the people of Nutwood, led by Rupert the Bear, are going to be fighting back.

Rupert, together with Edward the Elephant, Bill the Badger, and Pong Ping the Pekinese Dog will be stopping the bulldozers. The Wood Imps will be joining in the protest. And the Goblins will be there, getting pissed and throwing empty Tennants Super cans at the old Bill.

But things are getting worse. They are planning to knock down the House on Pooh Corner so that they can widen the road to make way for big lorries. And the river where Winnie the Pooh and his pals play Pooh Sticks is being polluted by industrial waste from nearby factories. And Eeyore the donkey has been depressed all these years for good reason. He has been depressed because he has been worrying about the hole in the ozone layer. Every day he is out in his field peacefully eating the grass. All of a sudden he looks up at the sky and he sees the tiny hole getting that little bit bigger. But recently he has started thinking about the current government. As a result he is getting so low and his friends are getting really worried about him. They are trying to reassure him that we can still get rid of the government and have a revolution. If we work at it.

And poor Christopher Robin. His father thinks that a growing lad should stop talking to Teddy Bears and think of a sensible career, like joining the army or joining the

Government. So he is taking Christopher to see a psychiatrist. The psychiatrist thinks that a round of ECT will shake Christopher out of his delusionary behaviour. Thinking he can talk to Teddy Bears. The fact is that Teddy Bears make more sense than some humans. Christopher Robin now lives in a Richmond Fellowship Hostel. And Marjorie Wallace from SANE will be on television saying, "how can we help people like poor Christopher who talks to Teddy Bears?" *Let him talk to Teddy Bears, you silly fool.* But the people of Nutwood, led by Rupert the Bear and his Posse, and Winnie the Pooh and his pals, are joining forces. They have even persuaded Eeyore to come along. The Wood Imps and Goblins will be coming along too. They plan to rescue Christopher Robin.

*   *   *

However, things are never without incident. As they start making their way through the woods, a jar of honey sits smiling at them from under a tree. One of the wood imps shouts out, "Look: some honey; how strange!" Of course, it doesn't seem strange to Pooh Bear, who rushes over to the jar of honey. Rupert rushes up to him. "Leave it Winnie," he says. "We've got to get to Christopher before it's too late. Besides, the honey might be spiked and you don't normally see a jar of honey under a tree in the woods."

This fact didn't seem to register on Winnie. It was honey; that meant food. He said to Rupert, "don't be such a spoilsport; Pooh Bear needs to eat, yum yum." So he takes the lid off the honey jar and puts his paw in. There are a lot of slurping noises. Then a big burp. And Winnie has just finished off all the honey. Then he starts glowing a purple/green glow. The honey was spiked alright; in fact it was magic. Then there was a loud roar. The earth shook. The trees shuddered. There Winnie was, standing there, six feet tall and extremely wide. Eeyore sighs and says "I knew this would happen; we will never get to Christopher now." "I should have stayed in my field." Then Winnie picks up one of the Goblins who has just opened a can of Tennants Super. In shock he spills half the lager on the ground. Then Winnie growls, "You mocked Pooh Bear, you called him stupid; you said he didn't have a brain. Now Pooh Bear will get his revenge." The Goblin, who is normally a fearless type, terrorising his neighbours in the woods with loud Punk Music, is now shit scared. However, he manages to compose himself and says, "cool it, mate; we're all in this together; we've just got to rescue your mate Christopher from those scumbag psychiatrists."

This registers with Winnie. He drops the Goblin on the ground and roars again and says Pooh Bear will fight psychiatry.

Off they all tread again. Pooh Bear up-front stomping along. Eeyore trudging along behind everyone. Sighing, he says to himself, "I knew this would happen. We will never get there now; we will probably all get arrested." But deep in his heart he knows that he has to go on. The trees don't know what's happening as a Giant Pooh Bear comes stomping past. He punches the occasional tree in his rage, and Rupert has to calm him down. "Leave the trees alone, Winnie; the trees are on our side too."

They finally get to the Richmond Fellowship Hostel where Christopher Robin lives. It is one of those places hidden behind a tall hedge. Pooh Super Bear, as he has become known, knocks the gate down and they all tread on up the garden path. Then he knocks the fount door down. The warden looks up from his desk, glasses dropping to his nose. "What's going on here, then?" He says. He gets up from his desk to ring for assistance. But just as he is about to ring the buzzer, Pooh Super Bear gives him a big bear hug (just enough to hold him captive), while the others all rush in and rescue Christopher Robin.

While this is all going on, the friendly Martians, accompanied by the goblins, have all gone off to kidnap the psychiatrist who gave Christopher ECT. Then the Martians will be taking him off with them in their space ship, where they will perform experiments on him.

(They will be coming back later for Marjorie Wallace.)

To them it's a strange characteristic that some earth people have, inflicting pain on their own people.

And Rupert, Winnie, and the rest of the gang will bring Christopher back to Nutwood. Together they will fight to stop the motorway, and the shopping centre (with the McDonalds in it) from being built. They will fight to save the House on Pooh Corner. And to clean up the river where Winnie and his pals play Pooh sticks. Pooh Bear has now shrunk back to his usual lovable size. But being a Super Bear sure has helped him to fight back against the forces of capitalist oppression.

Now they will try hard to reassure Eeyore that better times must come. And Eeyore will smile shyly and try to believe them.

(This was written down, in its current form, in December 1996. First version made up at a gig in 1995. It was inspired by the last years of John Major's government, but still seems relevant to Tony Blair's New Labour.)

Head Games

LOVE?

Is there any way
That someone described as "ugly" can find love
Do we have to wait for a fairy with a magic wand
To change us into a stereotyped image of beauty?
Can we ever listen to each other's hearts?

Sometimes I think the ugliness is in other people's heads
A fear of accepting
That there are alternative ways of seeing life,
Of seeing each other,
Must we always play at being "normal?"

In *Beauty and the Beast*
The beast was raging angry.
When he first met Beauty
He couldn't accept her,
After a while
He started to come to terms with himself
He started to get in touch with his feelings,
But he had to change into a Chippendale
lookalike
Before he could be accepted as human.

A "monster" cries
Showing beauty
The Incredible Hulk rescues a child
from danger

Reaching out through his chaos
But still the army and cops attack
Even when he turns back into a confused human.

Is there any way
That those of us seen as ugly can find love?
Acceptance?
And understanding?
A place for our hearts to speak?
How can we communicate our beauty?

June 1994

Pretty Girl

She had a pretty dress
A pretty coat
A pretty face
And a pretty hairdo.
But nobody really liked her
She lived her life in vain
And all the social workers
Were patronising towards her
Because they said she had a mentally
Subnormal brain.

She could sing just like Kate Bush
She could dance just like John Travolta
But she never went to discos
She always danced on her own,
In that little club for backward children
Hidden away in the back streets
Safe from all people
Who didn't want to know.

She had a pretty dress
A pretty coat
A pretty face
And a pretty name.

But the boys never liked her
Nobody understood the pain
And all all the social workers
Were patronising toward her
Because they said she had a mentally
Subnormal brain.

Can't you see we're all wounded inside
But we never realise it
Until we crack up.

1979

These are the lyrics to a song performed by the Fighting Pigeons. The song has a chorus of 'Mummy, kiss it better', that the author didn't write.

A River of Tears

Am I the monster?
That I'm sometimes painted as being
Or am I just a man
Confused by a world of contradictions,
Sometimes my body feels ugly
So I give myself pain
Sometimes I try to understand true beauty
And I like myself again.

Caught between the need to be loved
And the want to be hurt
The guilt of being macho
And the fear of being sensitive.

Can we cry
A river of tears
Beneath our armour
Is the need to express our fears.

Am I the monster
That you sometimes paint me as being
I struggle to be in touch with feeling
The sun shone today
Reflecting through shady trees
I tried to be at peace
But a battle raged inside me.

It's tragic when abused people
abuse each other

When years of pain make us bitter

We shout and rage
Through our fear
Inside we suppress a river of tears.

Are we the monsters
We paint each other as being
Or are we just hurt people
Confused by a world of contradictions,
Only feeling safe when we wear our armour
Building hatred out of fears
Unable to cry a river of tears.

Always fearing
Always fearing
We become lost and lonely
It's tragic when abused people
Become abusers,
The war rages inside
It becomes more real every day
But a little rainbow started to shine
Through a sky so stormy and grey

We attempt to let go of our power struggle
To be feeling once more
To liberate the need to cry
A river of tears.

Am I a monster
Or just a man
Struggling to reach his sensitivity?

January 1993

Seeing and Knowing

I saw a drunk
reach out his arms in acceptance
then smash a cider bottle
and fall to the pavement
calling out to passers-by
for a few pence
in a voice
worn away
by many years of cold weather.

I saw men in top hats
get out of limousines
just a few streets away
and tourists took photographs of monuments
that crumbled with the empire
that they grew in.

I saw a mother
being dragged away
from her loved ones
screaming for her rights,
I heard mental health authorities
sat in an office
planning the rest of her life.

I saw a child
trying to attract its mother's attention
in the middle of a busy shopping crowd,
I saw the mother
half-conscious
under a weight of worries
turn round and smack that child.

I saw the child
growing up confused
doctors called it 'schizophrenia'.
I heard baffled brains
trying to work out ways
to control a waking civilisation,
in a moment of peace
I saw sunlight shine
through a crack in a dirty window.

I saw a relationship fall apart
because the man
had become impotent
through his medicated mind'
I heard that mind
in loneliness and frustration
turn to thoughts of disturbance -
things that man never desired.
I heard his father
tell him about the evils of women
and how to live
a strict sheltered life,
I've heard all about you swinging couples
in the suburbs,
with your sex-therapy
and your liberated lives -
these things seem so uncaring sometimes.

I saw a tramp
being woken from his shop-front shelter
and sent out into the pouring rain
I saw the liberators
singing their songs of freedom
from the safety of a discotheque stage,
in a moment of dreaming
I saw kindness and peace

reflected in an angel's face.
I saw a tree
growing out the concrete,
I heard it laughing
as it gave off oxygen
to keep an uncaring city alive,
I first noticed the beauty
in the sky
and all of nature
when my sanity slipped
and I lost control of my mind.

I saw you
holding out your arms to comfort me
and I knew a little love
was still left in this life,
can we use that love to help others,
can we build a better life?

August 1982

SOBER

It's no fun being sober
When you're used to being drunk
The cold light of day is harsh
The weather's always overcast
Still you strive to carry on.

Irritable
Tempers rise
Jittery
Shaking
Unable to fly
Thinking of chances thrown away
In a senseless drunken haze.
Crying inside
Frightened to show tears
Unable to understand
That crying is a sign of being strong.

We're tough guys standing at the bar
Hard men afraid to fall apart
Watching the stripper on the stage
Another drink to numb the pain.

"I've got to go."
"No; stay and have another."
"What you having?"
"Go on and have another."
"What are you having?"
"I'll have another."
"What you having?"
"I'll have the same again."

Angry men we stagger home
Drinking brings out the ass-hole

Drinking brings out the fool.
Lonely fantasies
An empty bed
Feelings of failing
That you can't accept
So often we fall flat on our faces.

It's no fun being sober
When you could escape by being drunk
Ignore the bruises
The hangovers,
The beergut,
Another pair of trousers that won't fit
And a button falls off.

Never again the morning after
Same again the following night
Hiding in a can of Tennant's Super
Hiding in the pub.

Can we look at a shattered life
And fit the pieces together again?

And a voice says
"It's better being sober,"
"To start the day with a clear head,"
"We drink to escape depression,"
"Drunkenness encourages more depression,"
"Depression is not a good friend."
"Hope can be hard to find,"
"But it's worth trying."

I want to wake up
And greet the morning sunlight.

August 1996

I'm Drunk Again

OLD POET

The old poet sits in a cafe. He smokes cigarettes and drinks cups of tea. Eats a cheese omelette, chips and beans, smokes cigarettes and drinks cups of tea. Capital Gold on the radio, the sound of boredom, and he says to himself "Is there anything new? Everything fucking regurgitated." He dreams of creating symphonies, but all that come out are bitter dirges. He watches fashions come and go, the new, the relevant, expressing sentiments that he struggles to relate to, he watches from the sidelines a cynical observer. The old poet sits in pubs, getting drunk, reeling out his memories to anyone who will listen. Sometimes he exaggerates a little; he needs an audience to impress. It helps him value himself. He tries to tune in to the here and now, but he finds himself sighing, and says "Is this what I fought for? Did I fight at all? Or am I full of bullshit?"

The old poet wakes with a hangover, he stumbles to the window to face the morning. He reaches out his arms to embrace the sunlight. He tries to catch a sunbeam that dances mischievously around the room, a divine light. Deep inside he knows he's not a failure, this is something he tries to tell himself. There's no need to destroy himself with cravings, lusting to be liked and accepted. He needn't cheapen his act to impress. He spreads his wings and starts to fly; he takes to the stage with dignity. The old poet rediscovers his youth, he learns from his wisdom.

May 1996

A Night on the Town

Urban Muse

The stop start noise of traffic
Disrupts the poetic flow
The roar of tube trains
The noise of loud speakers
"There are signal failures"
"Don't give to beggars".
Weary bodies going home to the suburbs
Pushing, shoving, sweating.

There is no love down here
On London's Underground
No poetic rhythm
Can I construct something new
Out of this din?

A drunk staggering about a tube train carriage
Disgusting the commuters with his vulgarities
Incoherent words of anger and frustration
On occasions that has been me.

Walking in the park on a spring day
Conversing with pigeons
As they wander round in circles
Noticing daffodils and crocuses in flower
For the first time in the year

The First buds on London Plane trees.
Shutting out the worries
That nag so insensitively
The poetic flow comes.

Poetry is the rhythm of the struggle for survival
Finding words for the fears
That are so hard to articulate,
Sounds
Anxieties
Hands conduct an untitled symphony.
Tongues of wisdom
Seeking words for the inexpressible,
Poetry is the rhythm of survival.

January/February 1997

A JOURNEY THROUGH THE PSYCHIATRIC CORRIDORS

They label themselves as normal
They label us as mad
But the effects of this ideology
Become a little too sad,
So many of us get lost
So many of us get forgotten
The soul struggles against so many years of assault

This is the road we wander up and down
This is the road we cadge cigarettes on.

They label themselves as normal
They label us as mad,
But our anger is our assertiveness
Not an illness we should apologise for,
Feet shuffle on hospital lino
Open mouths
Staring eyes
And institutionalised clothes,
For years we have been suppressed by psychiatric drugs.

This is the road we wander up and down
This is the road we cadge cigarettes on.

They label themselves as normal
They label us as mad.
So often they speak on our behalf
But so many stories need to be told
So we don't become the scapegoat
Of many comedians' jokes.
But we don't need this scorn

As we get lost in a psychiatric ghetto
Always seen as the problem
But right now we're looking for our voice.

This is the road we wander up and down
This is the road we cadge cigarettes on.

They label themselves
They label us too
And the do-gooders run their nice little charities
And the scientists dither about
Looking for that elusive gene.

But I think they fumble in the dark
So many myths can be seen through
Once you know
The rhythm of the spirit will be proud and strong.

Where is the road on which we seek freedom?
Where is the road on which we find our liberation?

August 1990

The above, written in 1990, was a reaction to the advertising campaign by a group
called SANE (*Schizophrenia: A National Emergency*). The advertising campaign
featured distorted images of people's faces with captions saying things like "He Thinks
He's Jesus: You Think He's a Killer"; "He Hears Voices; You Hear Lies; They Hear
Nothing," and "She Thinks You Want to Kill Her; You Think She Wants to Kill You."
I found the stereotypes on these posters extremely disturbing and damaging. What
are the people in SANE trying to hide? How can a group of people label themselves
as 'sane' and other people as mentally ill, just because they have a more authoritative
voice? A more recent SANE poster has a message that reads "You Don't Have To
Be Mentally Ill to Suffer From Mental Illness." A very subtle and damaging message.
Since writing this poem, I have written more, challenging SANE's viewpoint.
However, this was the first attempt to articulate things. I have also been involved in
various demonstrations protesting about SANE, and in this challenging their views. At
the same time, and as part of CAPO (Campaign Against Psychiatric Oppression), I
wrote to SANE comparing their stereotyping of people who have been diagnosed as
schizophrenic with racist stereotyping. They never acknowledged this point in their
reply. But somehow I didn't expect to be taken seriously. I also wrote to the
Advertising Standards Authority making the same point about SANE's stereotyping.
They sent three postcards saying they were looking into it, and then a letter trying
to justify SANE's right to display such posters and to use such images. We have to
keep fighting on. *August 1997*

People in
Hospital Grounds

Frank Bangay
1985

SHOCKED TREATMENT

The Ramones said "Gimme, Gimme Shock Treatment." We all pogo along; nobody cares what it means. It's a larf, hey hey feeling brainy punk. But on the psychiatric ward things were quite different:- no pogoing, no speed or glue. Just Kemedrine, Stelazine, and all those other things they say are for your own good. Out of touch? No; down on our luck, fucked up against our will.

The nurse who claimed to be a punk liked The Damned. The punk patient liked X-Ray Spex, and sang their praises on his clothes. The nurse said they were a load of crap. I didn't agree; I likes X-Ray Spex. The Ramones sang, *Gimme, Gimme, Shock Treatment.* Fuck; it's only Rock and Roll.

Me and my mates had ideas for a band called DAFT (Disabled Artists for Therapy), or was it against? We all thought of instruments to play, somehow they fitted our personalities. We invented a dance called the Psychiatric Trouser Press, based on the institutionalised trousers that came up around your ankles. The clothes that people wore after years in this place.

The band never happened, but occasionally there were hospital discos, and they were crap. They took place in a big hall with wooden floorboards, out-of-date pop records were played. We drank insipid punch.

Male nurses stood on guard duty. If you feel motivated, get up and find a partner. But no touching, no hanky panky. "We are watching," "We are watching." "Though you are miserable, do have a good time."

The Ramones sang *Gimme, Gimme, Shock Treatment,* everybody pogoed up and down. The "hospital" was never a nice place, electrodes plugged in and the damage is done. Some days I want to explode in anger and frustration. Are we really the sick ones?

Spring 1995

Previously published in *Pogoing, Gobbing and Gratuitous Bad Language,* April 1996 and in *Dail Magazine,* May 1996.

The Ramones were a very inspired punk band from New York. Their first (eponymous) album, *The Ramones,* released in 1976, has inspired many people since then.

Footnote to *Shocked Treatment*

The Ramones were a very inspired Punk band from New York. Their first album, released in 1976, inspired many musicians from the Punk era and beyond, probably as much as the Sex Pistols did. They inspired me too. Their songs, being short (around 2-3 minutes), got to the point straight away. And they made many points too.

The song mentioned in *Shocked Treatment*: while not wanting to detract from the fun of the era, this was double-edged. It is sometimes good to send up the oppressive treatments within psychiatry, and poke two fingers at them. However, ECT (Electro-Convulsive Therapy) is considered by many to be very dangerous. It was discovered in Italy in the 1920's, and was initially used in abattoirs to stun pigs before slaughter.

The person credited with bringing ECT into use in psychiatry is Ugo Cerletti. He saw it being used in the slaughterhouses in Rome. The butcher would stab the pigs when they went into a coma, thereby avoiding the screams that a pig would normally make at a time like this. This method was used on the suggestion of the Society for the Prevention of Cruelty to Animals, as they saw it as being a painless way of killing animals. Cerletti went on to experimenting on dogs before using the process on humans.

In 1935, the first human was given ECT. He was aged 39 and an engineer, known only by the initials SE. He was arrested by the police while wandering round Milan railway station without a ticket, getting on and off soon-to-depart trains. The police took him to Cerletti for observation instead of sending him to prison. At the time, he was considered lucid and well-orientated; he said his ideas were telepathically influenced. Cerletti diagnosed him as a schizophrenic, and proceeded to give him Electric Shock 'Treatment'.

After the first round of shocks, the man burst into song. Cerletti continued the treatment at a higher voltage. The man then sat up and said *'Nona, Una Seconda, Mortiere'* ('Not again it will kill me') Despite protests from members of staff that if they continued, the patient would die, Cerletti proceeded. It is not known what happened to the man after this, as over the intervening time, the incident has been forgotten.

After this, ECT was used on people who were diagnosed as 'schizophrenic'. In its crude form it often produced epileptic fits. The idea then being promoted was that induced epilepsy was a cure for so-called 'schizophrenia'. Major tranquillizers, when invented, were given to people diagnosed as 'schizophrenic', while ECT came to be used more for people suffering from depression.

These days, in Western Capitalist countries, an *antithetic* is given when ECT is administered. In spite of this, many recipients of this so-called 'treatment' have suffered memory loss, and sometimes ECT can put people's lives in danger, as it can mean that the recipient of the treatment may not be able to return to a career that they previously held, and may find tasks that they were able to perform quite easily are now quite difficult. There have even been some cases of death while it is being administered, while it is considered by the 'experts' to prevent suicide. Some people have killed themselves after the treatment because of the effect it has had on them. I knew someone to whom this happened. So I have come to see ECT as extremely dangerous, and a subject you can't really joke about.

Sensationalisation of so-called 'madness', and painting a derogatory picture of it, runs through all forms of popular culture. And the Ramones may have had some understanding of ECT. Another of their early songs, *Teenage Lobotomy*, came from the time when wayward schoolchildren in the USA were being given lobotomies to make them conform. So, while I enjoyed listening to the Ramones, and saw how important they were at the time, I found I got frustrated with people who say the song as a joke, because I knew the grimmer side of the issue, and knew that most people wouldn't listen if you tried to explain.

The Ramones are still worth listening to. Their records can be obtained from Virgin, HMV, Tower Records, and all good record stores. Information on the history of Electric Shock Treatment gathered from *The History of Shock Treatment* by Leonard Roy Frank. Further information on the use of ECT in slaughterhouses can be obtained from the Royal Society for the Prevention of Cruelty to Animals. An up-to-date list of books on the subject (and other issues in psychiatry) can be obtained from **Survivors Speak Out, Tel: 0171-916 5472**, and possibly **National Mind**.

With special thanks to Chris Reed, Librarian at the RSPCA, for information on electrocution in slaughterhouses

May 1998

Voices of Experience

A few kind words of understanding
can help to heal the pain
that psychiatric drugs
and electric shocks make worse;
it just takes a little time
to listen to somebody
and everything starts to make sense.

By why, my friend,
do we sit alone and suffer?
The struggle under psychiatry
is such a lonely struggle,
where the labelling man
sets out to break solidarity
and we grow to see ourselves
as the problem
that needs to be sorted our,
and our anger towards injustice
gets turned into guilt towards ourselves.

We have a language,
we have voices,
tongues and rhythms of dignity and self-respect,
a sensitive anger
finding the confidence to say,
"Yes, my oppressor, I am somebody.
 I really am,
 I really am somebody,"
no force will beat our lives out!"

So I have come to see psychiatry
as a controlling force
that denies me the right for self-expression
to come out,
that psychiatric drugs and ECT
are cruelty
like that inflicted on kindred spirits
all around the world,
and the mind gets so confused
and our willpower struggles on;
but once you label someone
as mentally ill, you will never understand
why they feel depressed
or so spaced out.

Knowing we are right
makes us stronger,
but a little knowing is dangerous
to those that control and dominate,
knowing the workings of the system –
all the little gadgets used to scare people,
and the fears keep growing.

They say it isn't proper for a man to cry,
but many a broken-hearted man
has turned his head in shame and cried
as tears watered in his eyes
and the fears grew inside.
But its gets confusing in the aftermath,
so hard to remember how it all began,
so hard to remember your name and identity –
just another label
and case-note file.
So we have come to believe

that psychiatry
is a power struggle
all the way down from the top,
with sinister consultants
competing with each other
to see who can create the biggest
atrocities,
and the domestics clean up the mess.

But you know there way ways
to fight back –
we have a language to express ourselves with,
we have voices of dignity
and self-respect,
poetry and song,
words, and tongues, and rhythms,
the music of gentle sobbing,
the music of a proud heartbeat
bouncing around a room,
breaking through shrouds
into the world outside,
a sensitive anger
finding the confidence to say,
"Yes, I am somebody,
 Yes, I am alive."

So now I believe
that long-controlling drugs
and electric shocks
are cruelty of a most savage kind,
they just drain the spirit
and block the ability to express our minds,
but the spirit will struggle to stay alive.

90

The professionals will come along
with their 'cures'
but I prefer the word 'healing'
I just want to be healed,
we just want to be healed.

Two lonely people
sit on a bench
talking and sharing experience;
no longer nervous, they talk
with confidence;
their fears give way,
a trusting begins,
together they find inner strength,
gently knowing in their hearts
that this is what love is all about.

December 1986

I sometimes write poems with tunes or rhythms playing in my head. You can't hear the rhythms of this poem so well on the page. When I wrote this poem I had a disco tune in mind with guitars playing over it, the kind of guitar that you often hear in African music. Were this poem to be put to music and recorded, the idea would be that people could dance to it in discos while hearing the subject matter of the lyrics, and hopefully finding a little understanding of what the lyrics are trying to communicate.

The poem was written as a celebration of the creativity produced by survivors of the psychiatric system, and the feeling that our form of creativity is as important as any other form of radical creativity. But the poem also attempts to show the similarities between some of the procedures used in psychiatry in Britain and other western capitalist countries like ECT (Electro-Convulsive Therapy) and forced drugging, with forms of torture and restraint used elsewhere in the world. (In the West the modern-day use of these so-called 'treatments', ie. ECT with Antithetic may be more sophisticated, but it also makes things more subtle.) And such so-called 'treatments' as ECT are used in a crude and more outwardly barbaric form (without the antithetic) in psychiatric 'hospitals' in Third World countries. *June 1997*

The Road to our Awakening

Somehow I am shattered
On the road back to "reality"
The glare of the sunlight hurts my eyes
It's a hard struggle getting out of this world of darkness
It seems too distant from the world we used to live in.

The mountain is high
It's a long steep climb
We try to climb it,
The valley is lush and green
We long to be there,
Brother, Sister, we won't make it alone.

Sometimes it's like waking from a deep sleep
We try to tell ourselves this is a "normal" life
In a world of intellectual men
Who say they have cures for our "ills"
And new names to give us
For each mood
Each state of mind.

Memories laugh as they blow in the wind
All those recurring things
As we try to get on with living
The sun changes its face and starts crying.

At dusk we become shadows
Always on our own
Brother, Sister, why do we always struggle alone?

Somehow we are trying not to be afraid
On the road back to "reality"
We set about our journey with freedom in our minds
Though our eyes see things a little strangely.

We try to find a place where we fit in with the crowd
But our struggles have changed us
We're different now
Nothing will be quite the same again.

They say laughter is an excuse for not crying
So we are laughing now as we try to fit in,
Brother, Sister, can we laugh and cry together again
On the journey forward to our awakening?

Spring 1983

GLIMMERS OF LIGHT

Hiding in the shadows we feel safe
The mind flashes back to happier times
Avoiding nightmarish memories
and a voice says
"There are glimmers of light, old friend,"
"There are glimmers of light."

Blank walls block out signs of future happiness
Still we look for signs
Thoughts fumble over regrets
Losses that leave emptiness
The longing to feel again
Anger
Sadness
Anything.

I took my turn at trying to save the world
But I didn't realise how fucked up I really was
I believed that I was made of rock
But really I'm made of china or something like that
Something that will break so easily
Into so many pieces
Sometimes seeming too fragmented
To fit together again.

Where is hope
On this journey through darkness?
We keep on searching,
We keep on searching.

Alone in a city too big for comfort
Too many people
Too much loneliness
The spirit gets lost
In the noise and clatter,
You can become part of the crowd
And fade into insignificance
Or you can express your craziness
And get singled out.

I seek spirituality
I seek peace and harmony
Where is true friendship?
Where is love?

Sometimes I want to escape from this
competitive age
But there is no sanctuary,
Just a return to the psychiatric ward
We pay a high price in our search for enlightenment
Sometimes we try to pay with our lives.

I hide from loneliness
In a cold but crowded pub
I numb heartache with too much alcohol
I stagger on in drunkenness
Unaware, uncaring for the consequences
I ease sorrow with a feeling of bloated nothingness
Tomorrow I will curse the arrival of another hangover.
Kindred spirit we search alone

Through a world of inequalities
We look for meaning
We look for healing
We reach for stars that twinkle in a magical sky.

Madness comes and we try to recover
With hopes of finding love and understanding
I am afraid to be alone in my searchings
We get pushed and shoved
And pushed and shoved
And then we explode.

Hiding in the shadows we feel safe
The world outside seems full of hostile images,
A darkened mind tries to relate to a blue summer sky,
The soothing green of trees before they
fade into autumn.

There are glimmers of hope
A voice keeps saying
There are glimmers of hope
So keep on believing,
One day your spirit will be strong again
One day your spirit will start dancing
Dancing
      Dancing
           Dancing.

January 1992

Autumn Night

Pieces of Ourselves

And so we wandered through this world,
a song or two to help us along,
a song that gave us pieces of ourselves –
fragile pieces of ourselves.

Partners in travel, we come and go,
sometimes so close in struggle,
sometimes so distant and lonely;
from time to time holding together
a love that might flower,
helping us to share pieces of ourselves,
sensitive pieces of ourselves.

and we searched
for something to believe in
through night-time city streets
and grubby cafes,
through the places we lived in,
the possibilities we escaped into
and explored;
sometimes panic gripped us,
sometimes we understood,
we talked and shared our loneliness,
sad and precious pieces of ourselves.

To the institutions we passed through
when we stumbled, we tumbled,
where they tried to stop our wandering,

where they conspired
and kept our lives so conveniently on file, and
we tried to grab bits back from time to time,
saying "I feel this life is rightfully mine."

Hurt and alone we picked ourselves up again,
and one we wandered
and our minds wandered even more.

Partners in travel, sisters and brothers,
some friends left and went elsewhere
to a world we can't quite understand
where they'll find a little rest
from the strain and stress that became
too much to cope with,
taking them with pieces of ourselves,
sad and frightened pieces of ourselves.

and on we wandered
and on we wondered
through many situations,
situations that took away pieces of ourselves,
and in moments of reflectiveness we wonder,
will we ever heal?
will we ever grow back together again?

I want to be a flower
that blooms in the summertime,
I want to be a flower
that can survive the winter chill;
the buds on the trees half open

in the spring warmth
wondering if they are strong enough
to come out and face the world,
but as time passes their strength grows,
encouraged by the warmth and sunlight,
they open up and flower,
giving back to us little pieces of ourselves,
peace of mind,
peace of heart and spirit.

And these years later, we look back and remember
sometimes reassured that we have survived,
and every so often the child inside us
feels strong enough to express itself.

And from time to time we might meet a kindred spirit,
someone whom we share so much with,
and we give back to each other
pieces of ourselves
and we feel so much stronger;
we give back to each other
pieces of ourselves
and we start to heal and grow back together.

In Solidarity, May 1987

A Love Song From the Wasteground

All the leaves are turning brown
And falling from the trees
But through the silence the birds still sing.

Long faces sit in doctors' surgeries
Always waiting, never communicating,
       waiting,
       waiting,
       waiting,
       waiting,
My mind's not really sick,
I'm only imagining it.

Old ladies wander down the High Street
Shopping away their pension money.
Faded posters on derelict shop fronts;
Frozen faces never smiling;
Frustrated youths stand around.
In a world that gives you so little chance
You can't help but feeling let down.

Winter comes a little early
In some parts of town.

But see the people stood there staring,
Watching a tramp die in the road;
See the crowd of people all stood there staring
Watching the police arrest someone.
High on our foolishness

we learn our education in life
Out here in the street.

But the 'freaks' are out on parade
To entertain our intellect.
Hear the heckling
Hear the laughing
Laughing at us all.
We win another game by bluffing
But we win nothing at all.
Oh how the innocent fall,
Dead leaves to the ground!

Winter comes a little early
In some parts of town.

Doctors walk down hospital corridors
Under a sinister glow.
Nobody relates to nobody any more.
But we're all a little strange,
We're all a little strange.

And outside on the grass
Flowers bloom in spring
Opening our eyes to a feeling of beauty,
The grace of the night-time sky,
The glow of the moon,
Helping us to see.
The sadness lifts from our minds,
The tears flow from our eyes
Opening up into a warm smile,
Stepping out into a sense of light.

You know how it feels,
Don't you!

But down here in the darkness
Shaking hands hold cups of coffee
and cigarettes,

And we wonder why it's sensitive people
Who fall victim to the blows
Of this system
Always beaten Always beaten
Always beaten down;
Out here
Lost on this wasteground.

Winter comes a little early
In some parts of town.

But, the other day
I saw children playing in the park
Finding adventure,
Singing of life
and I lay down on the grass
And I listened to their songs of hope
And I forgot about everything else
And remembered love.

August 1978

FOOD AND SHELTER

So strange it is this world today
The old people walk up and down with the shakes
It's part of their illness it is said
But there is a different explanation
They have been caught in an oppressive situation.

Dumped in Victorian Institutions so long ago
Through situations in living that we know and ignore,
But psychiatric drugs are no solution to human needs
They just leave people to pace corridors
Broken and defeated.

All we needed was food
All we needed was shelter
A roof above our heads in hostile weather
A sanctuary to go to when times got tough
No, not these dark institutions.
Tell me,
Do you know the true meaning
Of the word 'asylum?'

So strange it is
So strange,
So strange,
The story repeats itself day after day
In a society built at a competitive pace
That wants to hide those who become seen as a disgrace
Because they find a more sensitive way of living,
But that disgrace reveals itself
In rejection and loneliness.
So you hide from the neighbours
Your 'backward' son;

So you hide from the neighbours
Your 'sick' daughter
Or so you call her,
But what have they done wrong?
Tell me, tell me; can you answer?

Some of us hide in hostels and lodging rooms
Lonely rides on buses to the next possible opportunity
Some of us get controlled by long-term injections
A community nurse to call
With a needle at the ready,
But drugs that control are no solution
To heartbreak and loneliness.
All we needed was food
All we needed was shelter
A roof above our heads
To keep us dry and warm
A friendly arm around us
To comfort us
When times got tough
And we lived with impossibilities.

So why do you take me here, to these dark institutions?
Tell me, do we ever think about the true meaning
Of the word 'asylum'?

So strange it is the way we stigmatise,
So strange it is the way we categorise,
Keep away from those funny people
"They're different from us," the crowd all say.
But did you ever look into my eyes
And see the fear I'm feeling?
Well what can you say?
That funny person might have been your friend
In a different time and place
It's just that situations make us change.

So strange it is,
So strange,
So strange,
We look for a fault inside the person
And ignore the situation.

But the ghetto just changes to suit the times
And the image of the mad person becomes so stereotyped
But it's much easier to control a rebel that way
As we do our funny little walks down endless mazes,
But how did we get to be here in the first place?

All we needed was food
All we needed was shelter
A roof above our heads in stormy weather
Someone who was understanding
We could have understood each other's needs.

So strange this world today
So strange indeed.

August 1985

The above poem, written in the summer of 1985, relates to some of
my personal experiences during the period of 1976-1978, and also experiences
of other people whom I knew at the time. It is to do with the revolving door system
that we can get caught up in once we enter the psychiatric system as a 'user'/recipient
of the services. Too often decision are made on our behalf and we can end up going
back and forth between hospital and hostel without there seeming any way forward:
what survivors used to refer to as the *web of psychiatry*. When we are discharged
from a psychiatric hospital, we can often return to the situation which caused our
distress in the first place (whatever that distress may be). Where is the road forward?
It is true we get food and shelter in a psychiatric institution, but we also get
labels which can prove to be very disempowering and single us out of society.

The original meaning of the word 'asylum' was place of safety, place of sanctuary.
This can be at odds with some of our real experiences of the psychiatric system.
July 1997

The Lonely City

AND THE WALLS THEY DO LISTEN

The walls have ears
They're listening in
You had better not talk too loudly
So I talk in silence
With myself
In conflict,
In confusion.

Forever restless
Forever wandering
A lonely road
That seems endless
Up
    And
        Down
            Psychiatric corridors
Begging cigarettes when I have no money,
It's just another day.

So many people here
But communication seems superficial
Together
    But
        Alone
            With
                Our
                    Labels
The woodwork gives off weird vibes
Difficulty in expressing yourself
May well be seen as an illness

They say you will never get better
They never listen.

But the walls are listening
Hidden tape recorders
I know it so well
They say I'm deluded,
But the consultant he knows everything
At ward rounds he seems awesome
and I know nothing
But somehow I understand too much for comfort.

Drugs trolley comes round
Three times a day
No escaping
A slow poisoning,
Strange things happen to our bodies
A cruel joke
Extremely frightening
I struggle in desperation
To believe in my willpower
Survival of the spirit,
Still you tell me I'm deluded.

But the walls
They do listen in
Once strong
We crumble so easily.

Friends come to see you
They talk of the future
Unable to understand what is happening.
I retreat

I go inside
Things crawl across the ceiling at night
Ghostly figures appear.

Friends become distant
Conversations become harder
They give up in desperation
I retreat some more.

But the walls are bugged
The spies are listening
A room full of noise
Complaints go unheard,
Fear makes us keep our opinions to ourselves.

Two televisions on at the same time
Playing conflicting soap operas
I retreat to my bed
With a book of poetry by William Blake
Nurses take it away
"It's not therapeutic"
"You might harm yourself"
"Here on your own."
So I join in
And enjoy conflicting soaps.

But the walls they did have ears
Sometimes they still seem to listen
Psychiatry is not medicine
But control and suppression
Never a healing process,
Never a healing process,

Nurses carry out duties
And a pecking order goes on.

Where is logic
Where is truth
The walls spy
And survey our moves.
Sometimes I look back
Sometimes I laugh
I see absurdity
Amidst the horror,
I value what I have learnt.

Damaged
A little vulnerable
Surviving gives us strength,
I refuse to be a victim.

October 1993

Landscape 2

VISION PART 1

A little bedsit
A figure sits on a chair
Boring wallpaper
A transistor radio
Cider bottles by the bed
Running away
Running away from what?

Many sounds disturb the dullness
Of a Sunday afternoon
The top forty on the radio
"Greetings, pop pickers,"
Thoughts chatter inside his head
A fear of going to work the next day.
A brooding loneliness
Too shy to speak
Time ticks away so drearily.

But there is a vision struggling to come through
A poem
A symphony
A visitation in the room,
A warm human being to keep him company.

And
The
Struggle
Goes
On

And on
And on,
Running away
Running towards what?
A sense of madness
Or a little release
Voices say conflicting things.

So he takes a bus ride to see a psychiatrist
In the outpatients' department,
Some tranquillisers to take
And something to help him sleep at night
He looks at pointlessness as he lies on the bed
The walls all around cut him off from the world.

A little bedsit
So dark inside
Running away from so many things
It's so hard to explain.

But a vision struggles to be expressed
A poem
A symphony
A love yearning to be embraced.

Warmth and compassion
Words of kindness
A poem
A symphony
A path to enlightenment,
He tries to follow that path.

August 1994

Vision Part 2

Some building bricks
A lego kit
Some pictures to look at
What does it all mean?

You're dosed up with medication
You can't think straight
So they tell you you're thick.

The psychologist says
"You have a below-average I.Q."
"With that and your history of mental illness
  You will never get a decent job."

But I came here
Because I have a fear of going to work,
A fear of noise,
A fear of dirt,
A fear of being bossed about and exploited.

I came here
Because my confidence was badly damaged
I came here
Because I was brought up to believe
That the experts knew best,
Now my confidence sinks some more.

I panic
I frighten myself panicking
I run into dead end corridors
Then I retreat into drugged despair.
Some building bricks
A lego kit
Some confusing pictures
I remember it well.

But I couldn't understand
I was depressed
Suppressed by medication
I couldn't think straight.

Hair grows longer every day
Beard covers face
Eyes peep out
I wear beads because they make me feel safe,
I lose my appetite.

Visions become vivid
Corrugated Iron fences
Spring up all over this dirty city,
Old buildings all toppling down
Lego land growing all around,
The barbwire is a side effect of the drugs
But a war is going on.

Ghosts drift across the room
Shadowy figures
A personal gloom
In fear I walk night-time streets
Lost and aimless.

But flashes of sunlight make surviving possible
Flashes of inspiration,
Flashes of genius,
The visions both create and destroy.

"You're pathetic"

The psychiatrist says.

"Pathetic and Manic Depressive."
"Such a personality disorder."
"How can we put you straight?"

"Are you gay?"

"Do you masturbate?"
"Do you take heroin?"
How do you get sexual relief?"

"The drugs make me impotent."
"I see."
"Very well,"
"Keep taking them;"
"They are doing you good."

I'm nervous
And working class
Without a very good grasp of Queen's English
I'm not very well read,
And at time like this I can never articulate.

Even some building bricks
And a lego kit
Confused me.

Rows of mushrooms grow in the grass
Butterflies flutter
Oh so fragile in the late summer.

Pigeons are overweight,
Corridors get longer
Corridors get darker
The further you go.

I wear a different face
And relate to new comrades
I embrace a false security
But the world's a frightening place
When you're alone.

Some building bricks
A lego kit
Some pictures I couldn't understand
Formed a gateway to this.

I survived
I learnt a little
Sometimes I feel able
To laugh in the face of mental
health labels.

Knock down those building bricks
Chant down Babylon
A reggae song playing inside my head
Brings the rebel out.

Yes, some of us have survived
And we're getting stronger.

August 1994

The above poem, written in 1994, relates to experiences I had in 1976 and 1977. After having a breakdown in the work-place (it was rather a dead-end job), I was given an intelligence test to assess my working abilities. This is not an easy thing to go through with when one is taking a lot of medication and is easily distressed. I found myself having my sanity questioned as well as my level of intelligence. The end result was for me to be sent, in late 1977, to live in a hostel where I was forced out every day to seek employment similar to the kind that led to the breakdown. Everybody living in the hostel was in a similar situation. The ideal dictated to people was that the best kind of therapy someone can get is to take their medication and do a hard day's work, the idea being that work, no matter how monotonous, is keeping your mind occupied, ie. one is seen as being well when working and ill when one is not.

Some of the imagery in *Vision Part 2*, like that in *Vision Part 3*, relates to how I saw London during this period. This was a time when a lot of London was being pulled down and replaced by new concrete complexes. In between times, a lot of wasteground sprang up. I found beauty in this. The line 'the barbed wire is just a side effect of the drugs' came from *Strange*, a poem which I wrote in 1977 and have since lost.

VISION PART 3

Sun shines on the waste ground
The rain has stopped
And the dark clouds have gone,
Weeds spring up through the rubble
And start to flower.

Butterflies hover over the weeds
Pigeons search on the ground for their daily meal
Beauty is created in this crumbling city.

Children play on the waste ground
Hiding amongst the mountains and the rubble
Playing Cowboys and Indians
With Cap Guns and Water Pistols.

Grubby face children
We seek adventure
Amidst the ruins.

Old Kettles, Fridges, Cookers,
Left here to rust with the changing seasons
Parts of our life
Thrown away
Used, abused and unwanted.

This city is a wasteground
Of lost hopes and broken dreams
Nature breaks free with sensitivity
Showing possibilities of growth.

Only to be cut down
And replaced
By concrete complexes
And tall towers of corruption and power,
The institutions where they take us
When we can't fit in no more,
The winter seems a little colder.

We meet on the wasteground
And tell our troubled stories
Of how our struggles wore us out
Now we wander up and down
And sit on benches
Passing another day,
Growing a little more grey.

We start to open up
Tears run from our eyes
Like rain from the skies,
They fall to the ground,
Weeds spring up through the rubble
And start to flower,
Showing possibilities of compassion and love.

November 1994

Wasteground

Stigma No. 3

My cause?
Well my cause
is to annoy you,
you with your false ethics
and taboos.

You see
I just can't believe these things,
I've seen too much
of the harm they cause.

My cause?
Yes; it's to make myself a nuisance
to you who sit around
saying "isn't it terrible
but what can you do about it,
all those poor people
and their misery?"
so we just let them scream in silence.

It starts with a joke about
a harmless little joke about . . .

You see
I believe in causing a fuss -
at least we can turn a head
here or there,
make someone think,
help someone on their way;
if that is being a nuisance,
then that is what I want to be

It starts with a rejection
of somebody
who doesn't walk on familiar lines,
somebody whose ideas
are not so conventional
as society would like,
somebody whose face doesn't fit.

Then the professionals come in
with textbook theories.

It starts with a joke about,
a harmless little poke about . . .

Label No. 1
is to make you feel put down,
not quite so good
as your so-called 'sane' friends.

Label No. 2
is to categorise you
as 'mentally ill'
so they can control you, or me, or you.

Stigma No. 3
Is to cut you off from society
as a deviant
who has committed no crime,
just spoken
his or her mind
about a situation full of absurd impossibilities;
but I'm sure you'll feel the strain
of living,
just like me.

Anyway,
what is a rebel?
and what are we conforming to?

My cause?
Well, it's through experience
not choice,
but it is
to keep on making a noise.
About our weird class ethics:
you see
I don't believe
that anyone is inferior
to anybody,
but I see the ways
we react to situations,
and the ways they condemn rebelling.

My cause?
Well, it is to keep on believing
that people can rid themselves
of the image
of being thick,
with support
and encouragement.

But you hear those theories
about somebody's inferior sperm,
the guilt and the shame
dumped on to
those who are born poor;
it's an ancient myth,
it's just practised more subtly now.

My fight
is to smash the myth
of mental illness.

It starts with a joke about,
a lot of gobbledegook about . . .

First they bring on someone
less able to be articulate,
then they tell them
that they are illiterate,
then they bring on the psychologist
with a smiling mask
and a pat on the head
and a sweet to suck -
"There's a good boy."
"There's a good girl."

First it starts with a joke about,
a harmless little poke about -
"HA HA."

Label No.1

Go on, dump on someone,
I know it makes you feel good,
I'm sure you can cleanse your conscience.

Label No. 2

Is meant to control you
with a label of 'mental illness'
and token gestures of niceness;
but I'm sure you can see,
through the mist,
one or two truths
refuse to be covered up.

Stigma No. 3
Is meant for all humanity -
at some time in our lives
things won't work quite right.

First it starts with just a little joke about,
a dig and a poke about.

Aim 1
Don't be put down.

Aim 2
Pick yourself up off the ground.

Aim 3
Believe in yourself.

BELIEVE. BELIEVE.

Go on!
         Believe in yourself.

January 1985

The above poem, about Psychiatry and the Class Struggle, was
partly written from personal experience. It was also inspired by
an article I read in 1984, which stated how, in America in the
1950s, psychiatrists were saying how slum-dwellers, ie. people
from ghetto areas, were less intelligent because they were born
from inferior sperm. This theory is classist and racist. It also
fails to take into account issues like poor housing conditions,
bad education, or lack of access to opportunities and
information. These theories are still very common in psychiatry
today, an example of this being the way black people are often
viewed by psychiatry. *July 1997.*

126

AND WE CAN LEARN

Children playing in the street
On the common
On the bomb site
Cowboys beating Indians with cap guns
Reading war comics
And the Brits always won.

But there was always one of us
Who never fitted in quite right
At an early age we learnt how to stereotype.

"Come in at once; your dinner's getting cold.
  Your father's got something to say to you.
  He's going to teach you a lesson or two."
"But we are not like those people
  Who live down the balcony
  You can hear their father shouting, oh so loudly,
  As he beat his children
  And they started screaming."

Roger the Dodger sometimes seemed wise
With his philosophy on how to shirk and skive
But his father had a big moustache
A slipper in his hand

And his shirt sleeves rolled up.
No matter how he tried
There was one situation Roger couldn't get out of.
The early 1960's
A new council flat
More room here to swing the cat
A bath with water running hot and cold
It will be a few years
Before the cracks start to show.

And though we came
Up from being poor
We harboured fears of black people
And considered ourselves unlike those people
On the other side of the wall
The mental people is what they're called.

The mental people
The mental people,
I became one of them.

August 1996

And We Can Learn, like the other poems in this book relating to childhood issues, is a fragment/snapshot. It relates to growing up in a working class area of London during the 1960's and looking at what was going on around me. This poem looks at the prejudices we learnt to accept.

Many white adults of that period, having suffered through the Second World War, held the misguided view that they built this country up, so that people from the Caribbean could come over and take all the job opportunities (a view exploited by the racist parties), when in fact Commonwealth people were encouraged to come over by politicians like Enoch Powell, and used as cheap labour, as were Irish immigrants in the 18th Century. Some people from the Commonwealth fought for Britain in the Second World War, a not very well-known fact.

These prejudices were very evident at the Secondary Modern School I went to and the environment I lived in. On leaving school at the age of 15, I found this prejudice very evident at the Labour Exchange, where black people were discriminated against in work opportunities (crap as the work might be). At the same time, I faced a lot of contradictions because, despite a brief period in 1969 of being taken in by the snobbery of Progressive Rock (a lot of it soon became pompous), I liked the black music of that time, including the Ska/Reggae that came from Jamaica. At the same time I held the prejudice/fear that a lot of people had towards the Caribbean families who were moving into the area that I lived in (All this is subject matter for a future poem). In my early twenties, through looking for work I took on employment in the Health Service as a Hospital Porter, then as a Hospital Orderly. Here I worked alongside people from the Caribbean and got to understand how hard these people worked, thereby getting away from the myth I grew up with, that these people were lazy and scrounging off the Welfare State. During this period I also experienced depression and started taking tranquillizers, which later led on to a dependance on anti-depressants and seeing psychiatrists on a regular basis. This later led to a breakdown and hospitalisation. Through this I learnt what it was like to be prejudiced against and stigmatised. I started to meet more black people and while I don't want to be idealistic, I started to see things differently.

September 1997

129

THE GNOMES IN BATTERSEA PARK

The Gnomes smiled in Battersea Park
Fairy lights twinkled in the trees
As a child I found sanctuary here
Away from the harshness,
The dirty city.

As a special treat
I was taken to the funfair
To ride on the dodgems and the big dipper,
The Drunken Sailor staggered about so absurd
The Laughing Policeman
Hit you over the head with his truncheon.

Drinking Chocolate,
Wright's Coal Tar Soap,
The Toucan on Guinness adverts.

I taught the Budgerigar to swear
But I didn't care
I wanted to be a punk,
Just like my hero Dennis the Menace.

The Gnomes got up to mischief in Battersea Park
Glow-Worms and Fairy Lights lit up the trees,
And reflected on the River Thames
A secret place in run-down Battersea.

Children are often seen and not heard

But they are often presented with many adult horrors
The disciplines that keep us in line
The beatings that knock us into frightened
aggressive adults.
Fucked up
We all struggle
To keep an accepted image
To escape poverty.

We win
We lose
We breakdown,
We scapegoat,
Sometimes feelings get shut off.

"Close your mouth when you're eating."
"Hold your pen properly."
"Stop crying,"
"Or I'll give you something to cry about."
As a child I could never conform to these things.

But the Gnomes played pranks in
Battersea Park
A Fairy Land in the inner city,
Candy Floss,
Fizzy Drinks,
Ice Cream,
Things that make a child's eyes glow

All those little buzzes.
Paper Rounds
And hard-earned pocket money
Factory smells that you leant to accept
The grit and grime of childhood.

Delicious Bread Pudding a penny a slice,
Dripping sandwiches,
The Bash Street Kids,
Desperate Dan,
Colonel Blink,
Rupert The Bear,
A little Childhood mischief.

And the Gnomes laughed in Battersea Park
I explored a magic summer evening,
The Gnomes smiled in Battersea Park
As a child this would make me happy.

late March/early April 1995

The Battersea Park Funfair was in existence until the early 1970's, when it closed down. The above poem relates to happy childhood memories of that place from the late 1950's and early 1960's. All these years later, memories have turned it into a magical place with tree walks, glow worms, fairy lights, and much more. The streets directly around the park were always quite well-to-do. However, elsewhere Battersea was always a working class area. The stretch along the river Thames to the east of the park, known as the Nine Elms, was always quite industrial. The same was true of the stretch along the Thames between Battersea Bridge and Wandsworth Bridge. Here the combined smells of the factories came to be known as the Battersea smell. On a good day it could be smelt in Hyde Park. A lot of Battersea has now changed and much of the industry got pulled down in the early 1980's and the property developers moved in. A lot of the river front now looks very different. However, Battersea Park, and especially the Funfair, brings back fond memories from that earlier period when I was growing up.

September 1997

A Cosmic Issue

Stars twinkle so clearly tonight
the endless cosmos opens up its highway
windswept hills where little folk wander
and chalk horses graze.

The restless spirit breaks rules
longing to seek
longing to discover.

The gnomes are having a party tonight
living it up in their own way,
laughing and chuckling
and having fun.

Cats sit amongst the Gnomes
and look up to the heavens
as they join in the celebrations,
and I wonder
can I tune in?

Foxgloves grow by the roadside
getting moisture from a little mud,
still they stand proud and beautiful,
little bird spirits hopping from branch to branch
wild Geraniums, Stonecrop, Lavender, Snow
in Summer.

The Gnomes are having a party
elves and fairies join in the fun,
mischievous faces of Tiny Teddy Bears
waiting for the television to be turned on.
And I wonder
can I join in the celebration?

Winnie the Poo and his pals are out in the garden
look: here comes Rupert the Bear and his mates
up from Nutwood
they're all sitting around with the Gnomes
smoking a peace pipe.
I wish I wasn't such a pessimist
I really would like to join in
because a child's adventure waits.

The sky is so clear tonight
you can see the stars
and the moon doesn't hide.
a restless wanderer breaks free
and travels the cosmic highway.

Fields and hills
mist and sunbeams
why is it so hard
for the spirit to be at peace?

The Gnomes are having a party tonight
hey, come on, join the rave,
to return tomorrow
to their place in the cosmic plan,
no hangover
just smiles on their faces,
and we all return to our worries.

July 1994

Footnote to *Cosmic Issue*

Stonecrop *(Sedum Acre)* is a succulent plant with sprawling stems covered in tiny leaves ranging in colour from light to dark green. In the summer it is covered in small yellow flowers. Its natural home is in the mountains of North Africa and Europe. However, it has naturalised itself in Britain, where it grows as a rockery plant. It can also be seen growing out of cracks in walls and on sandy beaches. I have also seen it growing it growing out of Tarmac in the Borough of Hackney, North East London, and in the mud, between the cobblestones, in Thirsk. North Yorkshire, where most of the inspiration of the above poem comes from.

The Sedum family is vast, and contains succulent plants, growing from Iceland to Peru. There are many species from the mountains of Mexico which are grown indoors in succulent plant collections. There are many others from the mountains of North Africa, Europe, Asia, Japan and North America, including *Sedum Spectabile* (Japanese Stonecrop), often called the Ice Plant (the true Ice Plant being *Dorotheanthus Bellidformis*, known as the Livingstone Daisy, form South Africa, called the Ice Plant because of the icy appearance of its leaves. These are members of the *Mesembryantheemaceae* family, a relative of the Living Stones, so called because they resemble the stones that grow around them in their arid desert habitat in South West Africa. In doing this, they camouflage themselves from animals in search of food, until their attractive flowers give their identity away. These Sedums, like the *Sedum Reflexum* and the previously mentioned *Sedum Acre*, are grown outside as rockery plants and, along with a few other species, grow wild in Britain, in mountains, moorland, coastal regions etc.

Snow in Summer *(Cerasitum Tameotsum)*, a plant of Southern Europe and Asia, is an alpine plant that is also grown in rockeries. It has small grey hairy leaves on sprawling stems. In the summer it is covered in white flowers, hence the name. It also grows out of cracks in walls, as it was doing in Thirsk.

SOLIDARITY

I cried
last night
but my
tears
were a mirror
of the
sadness
in the
world,
the earth
throbbed
loudly
a strong
beating
heart.

A tree cried
last night,
its leaves
drifting
downwards
in the
laughing
wind,
a tree bled
last night,
when someone
cut its bark
and let
its sap
flow freely.

And we stood
under
the stars,
our fragile
bodies
swaying
in the wind,
we counted
the years,
and shared
experience,
we were
cleansed
of pain.

We cried
together
last night,
but our tears
were
in solidarity
with
the sadness
in the world,
and through
our tears
we found strength

**OCTOBER
1982**

136

A Path to Light

The sun smiled today
Even though it's wintertime
A little unprepared for the chill
I stepped outside

A Pelagonium and Echeveria
In a pot on my balcony Still flowering despite the cold.
Memories of bygone summers
Those moments
When the warmth is in harmony with your emotions.

The moon smiles tonight
No longer angry
No longer macho
Sitting in the sky
Showing his effeminate side.
The moon is a wise old man
Somewhat saddened by the tragedies he sees
He watches wars take place on earth
So much suffering.
Saying I could light the way
AS you travel through much darkness
I could lead you on
To another dawn.

A dawn of hope
Hope to find
A path to lite
Don't give up
Don't give up
Don't give up the fight.
Keep on travelling
The journey to find
A path to daylight.

And the sun smiles a little
Saying 'I will return soon
To help create springtime.'

Bygone days
And
Future days
In the bleak mid winter we struggle on
As Jack Frost plays his icy pranks
Laughing at us
Always laughing.
In time he will retreat
As quickly as he came
Sun and moon working in harmony
Saying 'why can't humans do the same?'

December 1997

In relation to the two plants mentioned in the first verse of this poem: *Pelargonium* is the correct name for the summer bedding plants we normally buy as Geraniums. These are closely related to Geraniums, as both come from the *Geraniaceae* family. However, true Geraniums look quite different, with less succulent, segregated leaves. They come from Europe, North Asia, North America, Australia and New Zealand. Some species are hardy British garden plants, surviving English winters. A few species have naturalised themselves in England. The Pelargonium, however, comes from semi-arid and mountainous regions of South Africa, with a few varieties in countries like Spain and Turkey. Many of the wild species are very succulent, with swollen bases (known as *Caudiciforms*), or succulent stems and leaves. The shape of the leaves and flowers give their true identity away. If a cultivated variety is left to go wild, it will take on a more succulent identity. Other Pelargonia include the scented Geraniums, the most popular being the Lemon Geranium. Because of their habitat, they can survive a mild winter in a garden, and indeed, if given a little protection, quite a severe one. However, the combined cold and damp of an English garden may kill them off, especially the young plants.

Caudiciform succulents, of which there are many species, are able to store water in their swollen bases during drought. Other succulents store water in their stems and leaves. In their natural habitat they experience bush fires. The *Caudiciform* will be growing either wholly or partly under the ground and will be storing water, so that after the fire, when the rain comes, new growth will spring up. In cultivation, caudiciform succulents may well shed growth at a certain time of year.

Echeverias are a group of succulent plants from the *Crasulance* family. They mostly grow in the mountainous regions of Mexico, with some species also found in the southern United States and South America. All form *rosettes*, some low-growing, others growing stems, some of which sprawl, while others grow upright. Some have waxy leaves, others have furry leaves, while others again have leaves with powdery coatings. They come in many attractive colours: green, blue, grey, white, purple, mauve being examples. They also produce attractive flowers in orange, red, yellow or a combination of these. Most species produce off-sets very easily, and some can be propagated by just one leaf, which will root into the compost. A few species are used as summer bedding plants, although the damp of an English winter in a garden would kill them. However, they can survive a mild English winter on a balcony if kept dry. The species mentioned in this poem has quite large rosettes of blue waxy leaves (eventually shedding their lower leaves to grow up on stems) and orange flowers with yellow centres.

Enlightenment

A SPECIAL FRIEND

Won't someone please help me
Because I'm down on my knees
I may be boring
But I'm down on my knees,
I'm just looking for a friend
Someone to stay with until the world ends.

On an early spring day
We could sit in the park
Feeding the Pigeons, the Squirrels and Ducks,
On the same old bench
By the same old tree,
Listening to the joyous laughter of children.

But as evening approaches
It gets cold and dark
The moon starts to frown
And we feel so alone,
Always looking for a special friend
Someone to stay with until the very end.

(Made up at a gig in November 1993; written down in November 1994)

A Special Friend

THE SOUL OF A MAN

The soul of a man
longing to learn
expressing himself in the only way that he can
painting a picture of the world that's a little bit sad
sometimes painting with labourers' hands
sometimes painting with artists' hands
saying 'friend, please try to understand.'

The soul of a man
sometimes cries alone in the night
and on a dark day
he tries and tries
to be strong
and to stand up to those who keep him alone
in a state of confusion about where he's coming from
and he says 'I can be gentle and kind
and care for you friend
yes I will try,
so please lend a helping hand.'

And so he fights all that he is supposed to be
to try and be who he really is
to learn that being strong
means being sensitive
and able to cry
and caring
and being in touch with his feelings
and he tries to understand

And sometimes his emotions become
a little too real
and he's labelled by those who find it
hard to feel
their sadness
and their grief.
And on a troubled day
when the sun starts to weep

emotions struggle and will not go to sleep
and he says
"I love you friend;"
"Please try to understand."

The soul of a man
sometimes hurting inside
he remembers feelings that he tried to hide
the drunken states of mind
that helped him escape
from an aggressive world
the anger and rage,
coming home at the end of the day
to the hostile voices
that worried inside his head
he listens
and he says,
"Friend, don't they realise that they
   cause such pain?"

The soul of a man
and sometimes he tries
to suppress his spirit
but his spirit is strong
and the rhythm beats inside.

So he listens to the words of compassion
that he hears a few kind voices say
he listens to the childlike adventures
that he can sometimes relate to.

And he says
"You know it's true,"
"So friend, please try to understand."
"It's the soul of a man"
"And I'm coming through."

January 1990

Publications in which the Author has been featured

1. *Fear* (*Troubadour 2*, Troubadour Poets, late August 1974: Troubadour Poets held Monday night poetry evenings at the Troubadour Coffee House, Earl's Court, ed. Patrick Haynes. My respects to Dave Sheen, an inspiration from those days.)

2. *Spring is Rising* (*Springfield Words*, a magazine produced in Springfield Hospital, Tooting, South London, 1978, by Kieran Brown, an Occupational Therapist. I was a patient at the time, and helped him with it. In 1979 I helped to organise a half-hour of poetry and songs based round life in Springfield Hospital, featuring Kieran, myself and Dave Dorling who was also a 'patient' in the hospital. Dave sadly died in 1981. This was staged at the Troubadour. The gig was quite well-received.)

3. *They Say, They Say* (*Mixed Emotions, 1982* anthology, in pamphlet form, produced collectively by PROMPT (Promotion of Rights of Mental Patients in Treatment) Collective, of which I was a member, 1982.

4. *Woman on a Park Bench with Birds* (*Image and Words*, self-published pamphlet, handwritten, 1982.)

5. *The Road to Our Awakening* (*Hot Poetry No. 5*, eds. Dave Sheen & Frank Bangay, produced at a Community Poetry Group Meeting in Homerton Library. I was a member of that group.)

6. *When a Man Cries* (Self-published, hand-written pamphlet, 1984.)

7. *A Love Song from the Waste Ground* (*Sparks in the Dark*, anthology by Ignition Poets, based in Hackney Wick, late 1984, eds. Ed Simpson, John Lockhart, Hilary Porter, Diana Lockwood & Joe Bidder.)

8. *Illustration:* The Lonely City (Self-published, hand-written pamphlet 1985.)

9. *Illustration:* In Hospital Grounds (Self-published, hand-written pamphlet 1985.)

10. *Solidarity [Words and Image]* (**The Third Eye/ Psychic Issue**, magazine produced by Jay Ramsay, 1985.)

11. *Solidarity [Words without Image]* (**Radical Poetry in the 1980's**, anthology produced by Angels of Fire Poetry Collective, 1986, published by Chatto & Windus.)

12. *Stigma No. 3, & Seeing and Knowing,* (**What they Teach in Song**, a magazine of writings produced by CAPO (Campaign Against Psychiatric Oppression) Collective, of which I was a member, 1986.

13. *Pieces of Ourselves* (**The Cream of Troubadour Coffee House**, ed. Dave Ryan, 1989. A collection of poems by poets attending the Troubadour.)

14. *Pieces of Ourselves* (**The Rhythm of Struggle, the Song of Hope**, 1989/90. A magazine of articles, artwork and poetry from psychiatric experience produced by CAPO Collective. The magazine was an attempt to communicate both our ideology and our personal experience.

15. *Glimmers of Light; They Say, They Say, From Dark to Light,* anthology, eds. Frank Bangay, Hilary Porter, Joe Bidder; typesetting David Keys; Survivors Press, 1992).

16. *I'm Dancing with Damaged Wings* (**Kingsmead Voice**, now defunct local newspaper for Kingsmead Estate,Homerton, East London, where the author lives. 1994.)

17. *A River of Tears,* **Community Support Network Newsletter,** User/Survivor organisation based at Lambeth Accord, Brixton, 1994.

18. *The Laughing Flowers; And the Walls They Do Listen; When Words of Friendship are Spoken; Spring is Rising; Old-Time Friends.* **Also Illustrations:** *A Landscape with Someone Trying to Grow; Figure on Beach; Woman on Park Bench with Birds* (***The Long Road Forward***, self-published pamphlet, 1994.)

19. *Mad; Fear; They Say, They Say; In This Strange Land; Love; In Loneliness; A Special Friend;* **Illustrations:** *Hospital Ground; A Special Friend* (***In a Strange Land***, self-produced booklet, 1994.)

20. *A Journey Through the Psychiatric Corridors;* **Illustration:** *Hospital Grounds (rough version)* (***Under the Asylum Tree*** anthology, eds. Joe Bidder, Hilary Porter, Colin Hambrook, Jenny Ford; typesetting, Dave Russell. Survivors Press 1995.)

21. *The Road to Our Awakening; Love* (***Voices from the Heart***, anthology, ed. John Gaerty, published by Embroidered Dimensions, 1995.)

22. *The Laughing Flowers* (***DAIL*** [Disability Arts in London] magazine, January 1996.) *In This Strange Land;* **Illustration:** *Autumn Night;* (***DAIL*** [Disability Arts in London] magazine, March 1996.)

23. *Shocked Treatment (reprint);* (***Gobbing, Pogoing and Gratuitous Bad Language***, anthology of Punk short stories, ed. Robert Dellar, Spare Change Press, April 1996.)

24. *Vision; That Place on the Hill; The Gnomes in Battersea Park.* **Illustration:** *Spring in The Park.* (***Brixton Community Sanctuary Anthology***, 1996, eds. Paul Gerhard, Bushy Kelly, Amita Patel; typesetting, Dave Russell.)

25. *Solidarity; Words and Image.* (Sold and given away in various formats since 1982.)

26. *Stigma No.3; Food and Shelter; Voices of Experience.* (Sold as CAPO publications alongside our campaigning literature at Mental Health conferences, where we ran workshops, and at our fundraising benefits from 1985 to 1990. The idea that a poem from personal experience can drive a point home.)

Other publications in which the author has been featured, in Poems not included in this collection, include:

On the Streets (Troubadour Poets 1978).

Hot Poetry 1-4 (Produced by Community Poetry Group meeting in Homerton Library, printed on a Banda machine; eds. Dave Sheen, George Mitchell, 1980-83).

Voices, Feelings & Happy Spirits (Magazines of Poetry & Artwork produced by members of the Friday Club, St. George's Hospital, Tooting, South London: a social club for people using the Mental Health Services in the Borough of Wandsworth. I was one of the editors, and a member of the club from 1976. About five issues were produced from 1982-84).

Phoenix Collective (A Survivor-produced magazine on Mental Health issues, eds. David Kessel, Jenny Littlewood, Jan Wallcraft.)

Asylum (Magazine for 'Democratic Psychiatry'.)

Various articles and CAPO interview, featured in various issues from 1986 to 1989. (*Stigma No.3*, published in 1986.)

Survivors Poetry leaflet for Community Support Network benefit, Brixton Community Sanctuary, Autumn 1993. (Featured *Old Time Friends* on back.)

CAPO COLLECTIVE

People who worked on the publications

Eric Irwin, Frank Bangay and Barry were producers of *What They Teach in Song.*

Frank Bangay, Colin Hambrook, Elham Kashifi, Hugh Landsdown and Barry were producers of *Rhythm of Struggle, Song of Hope.*

PROMPT COLLECTIVE

People who worked on the publications

Julian Barnett, Frank Bangay, Cherry Alfree and Eric Irwin were producers of *Mixed Emotions.*

RECORDINGS

(Poems in this collection that were featured on record)

Memories by the Fighting Pigeons, 1979

1. *The Park Song* (with music).
2. *Pretty Girl* (with music).
3. *A Love Song from the Wasteground, 1979.*
   (without music; tape produced by Dave Boldinger)

Pieces of Ourselves, Poems of Experience

Self-produced Tape, 1989.

1. *Voices of Experience.*
2. *Pieces of Ourselves.*
3. *Solidarity.*
4. *A Love Song from the Wasteground.*
5. *Seeing and Knowing.*

The Road to Our Awakening

Self-produced Tape, 1990.

1. *In Loneliness.*
2. *Food and Shelter.*
3. *The Road to Our Awakening.*

4. *Tonight Faith Won.*
5. *Old Time Friends.*
6. *Stigma No. 3.*
7. *The Soul of a Man.*
8. *He Sees, He Feels.*
9. *A Love Song from the Wasteground.*
10. *The Park Song* (with music).

World Oyster Club Live at Bunjies

At the World Oyster Club, Bunjies Coffee House, Litchfield Street, London WC2. Sequenced by Razz; engineered and produced by Simon Scardanelli.

1. *Tonight Faith Won.*

EXHIBITIONS

1. *A River of Tears.* **2.** *In This Strange Land.* (**The Way We Look**, Exhibition, curated by Bushy Kelly for the Phoenix Appeal, 1994.)

3. *I'm Dancing with Damaged Wings.* (**Care and Control**, an Exhibition organised on the closure of Hackney Hospital in 1995. Featured on a video with images. I was attending an Art Therapy group in the hospital at the time.)

And thank you to all the people who bought a copy in advance, helping to make this publication possible. Your support has been much appreciated; also to the three kind people who made donations, and to Spare Change Books for their substantial financial assistance.

PUNK CONCERT, IN WHICH THE
AUTHOR TOOK PART

Hackney Anarchy Week & SPARE CHANGE BOOKS PRESENT

LAUNCH PARTY!
FOR

GOBBING POGOING AND GRATUITOUS BAD LANGUAGE!
An anthology of punk short stories

LIVE PERFORMANCES BY

ALTERNATIVE TV

(1978 set & surprises)

STEWART HOME
RAOUL 'BOREDOM' KALOWSKY
EMMA MCELWEE
FRANK BANGAY
FRIDAY 24th MAY
8-11 pm
CHATS PALACE
BROOKSBY WALK, HACKNEY

£3·50/£2·50 concs
MUSIC JOURNALISTS + BOOK CRITICS £6
AND WILL ONLY BE ADMITTED IN FANCY DRESS

THE ORIGINAL SOLIDARITY
POSTER FROM 1982
(*Now a Collector's Item*)

The Author & the Ship of Fools
At the Tate Gallery, London
Photograph by Colin Mahoney

A Weeping Tree

Some Words About the Author

Frank Bangay was born in the Borough of Wandsworth, South London, in 1951. He left school at the age of fifteen (though since then he has taken on various forms of Further Education). He has been employed as a factory and warehouse worker, a messenger for a shipping company, hospital porter, hospital orderly, shop worker, kitchen porter and gardener. He started writing poetry in 1972, and the following year began attending the Monday night poetry evenings at the Troubadour Coffee House in Earl's Court (a place he often frequented until its temporary closure in 1989). He also became involved in various community poetry groups around London, and in this period helped to set up a couple of poetry groups: Young Poetry, at the Centre in Charing Cross, then a club for young people, and Junction Poets that met in Battersea Arts Centre, when it opened as a Community Arts Centre in 1975. From 1979 to 1981 he worked with musicians in the Fighting Pigeons, who performed at various venues around London.

Frank is a survivor of the psychiatric system, an experience he first encountered in the 1970s. Creativity has always helped him pull through. In 1980 he became involved with the survivor movement in a group called PROMPT (Promotion of Rights of 'Mental Patients' in 'Treatment'). In 1985 they changed their name to CAPO (Campaign Against Psychiatric Oppression). As well as being involved in their campaigning and awareness-raising work, he also helped to organise many fund-raising benefits, through this helping to give voice to various survivor poets. He also helped to publish some magazines of writings by people who had shared psychiatric experience.

Frank was a founder member of Survivors Poetry. From 1992 until 1997, as a voluntary worker, he organised and co-organised many performances and workshops in Psychiatric Hospitals, Day Centres, Sheltered Housing and other similar settings around London, through this continuing to help many survivors poets get their voices across. He is currently helping to establish a Survivor Writing Group at CORE Arts in Hackney.

As well as performing around London, he has performed as far afield as Leeds, Cornwall and Dublin, and has performed on the same bill as punk legends Alternative TV. Frank continues to write and perform; he also grows many plants, including a large collection of cacti and succulents.

This is Frank's first collection of poetry and illustration, and took a long time and a great deal of ambition to come to life.

January 1998

Special thanks to Dave Russell for helping to make this collection possible.